Making the Connections

MAKING THE CONNECTIONS

Live the Life You *Really* Want

Elke Babicki

EPIGRAPH PUBLISHING
RHINEBECK, NEW YORK

Contact the publisher for information:
Epigraph
27 Lamoree Road
Rhinebeck, N.Y. 12572

Printed in The United States of America.

Library of Congress Control Number: 2007936956

ISBN 978-0-9798828-0-7

Bulk purchase discounts for educational or promotional purposes are available.

First Edition

10 9 8 7 6 5 4 3 2 1

The intent of the author is only to offer information of a general nature to help you in your quest for emotional and spiritual well-being. In the event you use any of the information in this book for yourself, which is your constitutional right, the author and the publisher assume no responsibility of your actions.

EPIGRAPH
A DIVISION OF MONKFISH BOOK PUBLISHING COMPANY
RHINEBECK, N.Y. 12572
WWW.EPIGRAPHPS.COM

Dedication

To Sasha, my daughter
and the generations to come

Acknowledgements

My gratitude for their early enthusiasm and consistent support goes to Sareeta Bahadoorsingh, Sherilyn Smith, Shirarose Wilensky, Gislinde Bronson, Jo Blackmore, Diana Douglas, Angela Pegg, Victoria Miachika, Cheryl Wheeler and Roxanne Thornton.

A special thanks to my publisher Paul Cohen and my editor, Cait Johnson for their deep caring and professionalism.

I can never thank my husband Matt and the rest of my family and friends enough for providing the encouraging and supportive background without which this book would not have been possible.

Table of Contents

Introduction xi

PART 1: The Reluctant Medium, A Psychotherapist's Journey 1
My Life and Calling
The Hummingbird
Navin's Journal
Synchronicity
The Magic Photos
All Happening Now: the Holograph
A Channeled Message
Tarot and My Psychic Great-Grandmother
The Real Meaning of After-Death Messages
It All Began with One Step

PART 2: New Paradigm 101: What It Is and How to Get There .. 21
The Paradigm Quiz
Building the Pyramids
The Fear Pyramid
The Freedom Pyramid
Living the Freedom Pyramid
The Magic Equation
The Network: Science, Interconnectedness, and Holographs
Sacred Geometry
Making the Shift
Steps on the Journey to Freedom
1. Breaking Out of Old Paradigm Roles: Bullies and Victims
2. Owning Our Shadow Selves
3. Good, Evil, and Free Choice
Bad Boys/Good Boys: Trusting Intuition
Misguided Beliefs
4. Claiming Our Sensitive Empathic Power
Grow Your Own Success Fund
New Paradigm Principles for Living
ACCESS: Acronym for Living the New Paradigm

PART 3: A Guidebook for Belonging 72
Stories as Healers and the Healing Power of Love
Bliss
My Bliss Experience: The Good Spot
Inviting Bliss In
Better Than Drugs
Bliss in Our Culture

Experience Bliss Yourself
Deep Dreaming
    Dreaming My Father's Death
    Decoding Dreams
    Dreams and Visions
Dream Deeply Yourself
    Write Down Your Dreams
    Think About Your Dreams
    Maintain High Ideals
Remote Viewing
    My Mother's New Habits
The Power of Manifestation
    Making Visions Real: The Dream House
    Manifest for Yourself
    Connect with Your Deep Soul-Desire
    Work on Knowing You Deserve
    Imagine in Detail
    A Formula for Success
Sensitive Intuition and Empathy
    Intuition in History
    Becoming More Intuitive
    How I Receive Intuition
    What Sensitivity Offers Us
    What Sensitivity offers the world
    The Challenges of Sensitivity
    The Task at Hand
Nurture Your Own Openness and Sensitivity
    Pay Attention
    Trust Your Gut
    Journaling
    Try Some Deep Seeing
    Nourishing Solitude
    The Color Exercise
    The Calming Power of Nature
    Dancing and Movement
    Theme Songs
    The Practice of Love
    A Word About Indigo Children
General Practices for Living in the Emerging Paradigm
As We Go Forward

BIBLIOGRAPHY.. 123
RECOMMENDED READING.................................... 131

Introduction

We live in a time of remarkable change: we are beginning to realize that our thoughts have the power to affect our reality. Books like *The Secret* are making us aware of the law of attraction and how it creates our experience, and many people are discovering the extraordinary transformation that results from opening ourselves to this revolutionary shift. I am certainly one of them.

When I started researching new-paradigm possibilities and how they differ from the old worldviews of science and religion, I made a discovery that changed my life: I tapped into an underlying network that connects all things. This network is so much vaster than the current ways of believing, and simply becoming aware of it moves us to a level of consciousness that is infinitely more adaptive and powerful. When I let this spark of consciousness ignite in me and began living my life from a new perspective, from a place of heart, I experienced abundant passion and energy, my writing became inspired, I began dreaming powerful predictive dreams, and intuition guided me effortlessly to where I needed to be.

The key to my own transformation was so simple. It was the decision to become more compassionate and empathic. I have become convinced that developing this kind of sensitivity is the crucial step towards creating a more positive and healed future for humanity. I learned from my own amazing experiences that doing so brings huge benefits to us as individuals, besides contributing to the wellbeing of future generations.

If you desire to follow along this path of intuition and vision, know that there is plenty of guidance, inspiration, and encouragement along the way. This book is part of that guidance. As I share my own stories with you—stories that may seem incredible at times, but which all actually happened—I invite you to join me on a journey of exciting discoveries that will greatly improve the quality of your life. In this book, I will offer some keys to energizing your mind, body, and spirit and some answers to life's greatest questions as those answers came to me on my own transformational journey. I invite you to let yourself be stretched, to be open to what may seem at times to be mind-bending phenomena, and to be open to possibilities. As Thoreau said, "Direct your right eye inward, and you'll find a thousand regions in your mind yet undiscovered."

PART 1

The Reluctant Medium: A Psychotherapist's Journey

"We must be willing to get rid of the life we've planned, so as to have the life that is waiting for us."

—Joseph Campbell

When I first met Sareeta, my new client, I was struck by her extraordinary beauty, with her honey-gold skin, long, lustrous black hair, and mysterious dark eyes. But despite her grace and dignified composure, it became clear in our session that she was in deep mourning for her beloved brother, who had been killed in a car accident. His name was Navin and he was 26 years old. Sareeta and Navin had been very close; she adored him and described him as a kind-hearted person who strove to do right by people.

During our session I had received a strong sense of Navin's presence, but it was a feeling I couldn't put into words at the time. I was feeling unusually moved by this and, not surprisingly, the image of Sareeta came into my mind before falling asleep that night. I felt a great amount of empathy and compassion for her, and a sense that there was something more here, that I had just touched the surface of something. With this I fell asleep.

Suddenly, during the night, I was startled awake by a very clear voice in my ear. The voice was neither friendly nor nasty but direct, businesslike, and impossible to ignore. The voice said, "This was an intercultural, interracial hate crime."

What does that mean? I thought. I was so drowsy I couldn't even process this strange sentence, and I thought confusedly, Okay, what do I do with that voice? "Don't panic," I told myself, trying to calm my racing heart, sweaty palms, and dry mouth, "just go back to sleep and deal with it in the morning."

When I woke in the morning, I knew something important had taken place. This voice was distinct. It wasn't just a dream or a delusion, not a figment of my imagination. I could still hear the same sentence, the same matter-of-fact sounding voice, impossible to ignore. This voice came from somewhere else. I felt I had crossed an invisible threshold into another world. On the surface, all was as it should be, my surroundings were the same, but I knew everything was profoundly altered. Although I wasn't aware of the magnitude at the time, I knew that somehow the course of my life had changed.

The first thing I did that morning was to tell my husband Matt about the dream. I just had to tell somebody and make sense of it somehow. Besides, I could always depend on Matt, my engineer/scientist sounding board, to be my reality-check. I told him about the experience, looking at him expectantly.

He gazed back at me in the bathroom mirror and thought for a few moments. I was wondering if he was going to reach for the thermometer to check my temperature. Instead he reached for the electric shaver in the bath cabinet and said, a little wistfully, "Well, this sounds different. It seems like an important dream, you should find out what it's all about."

"You think?" I tried to determine if he was serious.

"Well, I would," he nodded sincerely, "if I had a dream like that."

This answer, especially from Matt, really surprised me. But that was the moment I decided to ask Sareeta if the dream could have any relation to her brother. I couldn't think of anything else to follow up on.

Patience has never been my strong suit. I could hardly wait to get Sareeta's reaction, since I felt she could shed some light on the situation, so as soon as she was seated comfortably in my office, I started to ask her gently, apologizing beforehand for any mistakes I might be making, if the dream could be related to her brother's passing. When I completed my sentence, she looked at me with a stunned expression—eyes wide, mouth slightly open, composure in tatters.

Once she found her voice again, this story poured out of her: "I can't believe it! How did you know? There is an investigation into Navin's death! There are many crimes committed against wealthy young Indian men in Trinidad, and Navin drove a BMW, which would have given the appearance of wealth. The evidence at the scene suggests that he was speeding as if he was trying to get away from somebody. Of course, there were no witnesses. Many kidnappings take place there, especially in the particular spot where Navin was killed. The crimes are often racially motivated. People are kidnapped or murdered for money or just to make a statement. Greed and hatred are the primary causes for these crimes—and the police may be involved as well. Fear and confusion are everywhere. My family has little hope of finding out what really happened, especially since so many members of the police are corrupt."

I was stunned by this revelation; Sareeta had not mentioned any of this in our first meeting. I had had no idea about the interracial conflicts in Trinidad; to me, it seemed like an exotic place to visit and Sareeta seemed exotic herself, not like somebody who would be targeted for violence or discrimination.

It was in this session that I felt the back of my neck beginning to hurt badly. I wondered if this is what had happened to Navin in his final moments on this earth—I wondered if his neck had been broken. I had to check this out with Sareeta and when I asked, she confirmed that this had indeed been the case.

For our next session I wore an old sweater that I had not worn in a long time. It was royal blue, and I finished my ensemble with one of my favorite necklaces, made of moonstone. This immediately put a smile on Sareeta's face. "It's like I'm getting a message from Navin," she said. This kind of blue was his favorite color and he loved moonstone. Sareeta was feeling calmer and connected with Navin. She told me she was planning to bring in her whole family next. I was trying to take all this in stride, but I certainly did not want to feel like anybody was expecting me to channel Navin: I had never done anything like this before. But she assured me that all she wanted was for her family to meet me.

Then they came into my office, her father, grieving mother, and beautiful, sorrowful sister. There was a lot of raw emotion in the room during that session, and the pain was deep and present.

I felt that I was taking on the role of a medium reluctantly, yet I was somehow compelled to be there. I began getting strong messages from Navin. I could see him showing me the palms of his hands. I was still learning, striving to understand, and I could feel his impatience. He was trying so hard to get through, and I was struggling with a combination of resistance to this phenomenon and excitement. With all this, I started to develop a splitting headache. It was so hard for him to watch his grieving family, especially his mother. He could not bear to see her in pain. He began shouting through me, "It has not been a waste! Turn my death into a victory!" He wanted his family to realize that he has more power now than he did when he was alive. The beauty of his hands told me that he is doing important work now, doing the kind of healing with his soul that he couldn't do in his life. This was very important to him and he really wanted to let his family know.

Navin sent another important message: Death is just a transition. Dying is like going through scary rapids and coming out to a beautiful lake, and there are many people and spirits there to help. But Navin's most important message to all of us was that nobody dies alone. Most of all, he wanted to let his sister know this so that she could stop worrying; all he wanted for her was peace. He let me know that if he could just get his message to Sareeta, she could help the rest of the family.

After these transmissions, we simply sat together and felt Navin's consoling presence surrounding us with love—a love that had transcended time, place, and even death. Each of us felt blessed by feelings of a profound and loving peace.

My Life and Calling

So how does a respected psychotherapist with a consulting practice for employees of large corporations find herself channeling a dead man? This was certainly an experience I never expected to have. But now that I look back, I was being guided step by step along the path from the very beginning.

After extensive trainings in everything from Gestalt, family therapy, cognitive restructuring, and solution-oriented therapy to neuro-linguistic programming, I had worked for many years in the field of corporate business consulting and counseling for employees. After my daughter was born, though, I decided to concentrate on deeper work with individuals and began a private practice as a registered clinical counselor. This was a good compromise for quite a while, since it allowed me to keep my own hours, attend to my daughter, and keep myself involved and updated in my profession. But I began to realize that, although I had always benefited from my many courses and trainings intellectually, and received new energy and enthusiasm about my work from them, I didn't apply the principles very much afterwards. Instead, I slowly realized that I had been practicing my own brand of therapy, based on empathy and an intuitive understanding of what each person needed. Acting on intuition, I was able to reframe, support, or challenge clients, depending on what would help them to move forward with their lives. My goal was to get my clients to stand on their own feet quickly, and to help them find their own inner resources and passion about life.

Then something really shifted in 2004, my 50th year. I had become quite successful and accomplished in my career, my daughter was a teenager, and I began to feel that it was time to go deeper into what was possible for me to do. 2004 was the year I had a change of heart. I had been trying to summarize my approach and advice in a book, so that I could help more people and not have to keep repeating myself, but I wasn't really interested in the subject and I felt a sense of futility: it had all been said before. A small voice deep inside me kept insisting that I should go deeper into empathy and intuition and see what would happen. It was a bit like standing by the pool and not daring to jump in for awhile. Society's prohibitions against such "unprofessional" stuff as intuition was very ingrained in me; I was still holding on to the old linear paradigm.

Then one day, in a session, I finally jumped. My client was a young woman, a business referral. She was stressed and unable to get any relief from her constant anxiety. I noticed she had trouble breathing and slowing down, but no rational approach and no explanation of the adrenaline cycle or cognitive restructuring could reach her. It was then that I suddenly noticed a distinct smell, although there had been no trace of it before. At first I couldn't place it, but then I knew it from somewhere in my childhood: mothballs!

I took a wild leap into the unknown and asked her what this might mean. What happened next was completely unexpected: she broke down and began to cry her heart out. She told me between sobs, "It's my mom. She was the mothball queen—she wrapped everything in mothballs. She put together a trunk for me with all her treasures, and it is waiting for me in South America since she died last year. I'm sure everything in it will smell like mothballs."

As she worked through her guilt and grief for not having been there during her mother's illness and subsequent death, she began to feel real relief. Evidently, her South American mother had kept the seriousness of her condition from her daughter to ensure that her daughter could continue to build a good life for herself in Canada. My client felt guilty for not having known her mother needed her and she felt badly that her mother had wanted to protect her so. As we sorted through all the implications and assumptions the client had made, she felt cleansed of what had been bothering her all along.

That session made me realize I needed to start trusting this kind of guidance. I did not feel out of control—on the contrary, I felt more in control after this session. Throughout my professional career I had never thought of what to say next to my clients, but always trusted that I would know what to say. Now I began to have even more faith in inspiration. I felt that I had reached a new level of perception that could deepen the work and hasten the recovery for my client, and there was certainly nothing wrong with that. If the businesses couldn't handle it, I thought, then so be it. I resolved to simply stay open and observe what happened from there. I noticed that my feelings of empathy were growing stronger. It was at this point that Sareeta came to my office for the first time.

After the experience of channeling Navin, the inner shift began to accelerate. If I had held on to the old paradigm, so perfectly expressed in classical clinical psychology, then this unconventional but deeply healing treatment of Navin's family would never have been possible. The more I trusted guidance from non-linear sources, the stronger the guidance became. I gradually began relaxing into a new perception of the unity of all life. And the messages continued to come in.

The Hummingbird

One evening as I was speaking to Sareeta on the telephone, I looked out the window and saw a hummingbird at our feeder. It caught my attention because it stopped moving. Usually, hummingbirds move their wings very rapidly and touch down for their nectar briefly before flying off again. Not this one: it sat calmly and quietly while Sareeta and I talked. After a few minutes I mentioned this to Sareeta and she asked what color it was. I could make out the orange feathers on his head but could not see if the stomach was metallic blue or green. I wanted to come right up to it at the window, but thought the bird would surely see my movement and fly off. I decided to take the chance anyway and came very close to it. The hummingbird did not move. His stomach was a beautifully shiny deep blue color. I actually timed his presence then, since it was so unusual. The hummingbird sat still for about 10 minutes. Sareeta gave me another shock when she told me that the native Carib people call Trinidad "Iere," or "The Land of the Hummingbird." And of course, Navin in particular adored hummingbirds.

Navin's Journal

Sareeta is a social worker and also a deeply empathetic person; her compassion for children makes her perfectly suited for her work in adoptions. This empathy was part of the reason she could appreciate and feel close to her brother—and I think it helps to explain what happened for her after his death.

When she went to Trinidad for Navin's funeral, Sareeta woke up in the middle of the night because she felt Navin sending her his thoughts: "Look out the window," she heard, and "Journal."

She got out of bed and walked to the window in the dark room. At that point though she was too scared to look because she couldn't believe she was sensing the messages. A few days later, as she tidied Navin's room because she didn't want her mother to do it, her tidying became strangely energized, as if Navin wanted her to search for something, but she didn't know what he wanted her to find. She looked everywhere, even in the pockets of his clothing. She eventually stopped, even though she felt his energy telling her not to quit.

Then, the very next day, she unexpectedly came upon a hiding place—and there was Navin's journal. She was amazed: she hadn't even known he kept one. His first word in the journal was "Sareeta." Tears rolled down her face as she read it. She was grateful for that gift and felt honored that he wanted her to find it. She realized that it was intended to help her fill in the lost time of the years he was in Trinidad.

Synchronicity

In my own journey into the subconscious I kept making decisions to deepen in empathy, to develop open and accepting thoughts and actions rather than critical ones, and to choose loving thoughts over fearful ones. As a result, there was a corresponding difference in my own inner experience: I began to feel an expanding sense of peace and joy. I began to see and hear things and to receive answers to questions in ways which were much more powerful and satisfying than anything I had ever experienced under the old-paradigm, linear and rational way of being. I felt that I was tuning into a positive wavelength that I had previously misjudged, finally finding the ease and depth that I had always known were there but had been afraid to believe in. Rewarded and encouraged, I continued to expand my loving thoughts, actions and perceptions. It was a lovely cycle.

One fringe benefit of all this was a marked increase in synchronicity, which is such an effortless way to solve problems. For example, a book would be placed at eye level on a shelf with answers to a question I'd been asking, or I would think about contacting somebody and they would suddenly appear at an unexpected location. In fact, that was how I was guided to Cindy.

The Magic Photos

Cindy, a talented photographer, or visual poet, as she calls herself, had told me that occasionally she finds spirits appearing in her pictures, like the image of a deceased grandfather in the cloud behind his grandchild. I had always remembered that story and thought it might be helpful to call her in to take photographs of Sareeta. The only problem was that Cindy had been abroad for years and I had no idea how to get in touch with her. But, living in my shifting paradigm where synchronicities were happening, it turned out that I did not have to track her down. We bumped into each other as we were both shopping in the same store—in a town neither of us actually lived in!

So Sareeta, Cindy, and I met. Cindy took photographs of Sareeta in action, talking to me, and one picture of her holding her favorite photograph of Navin. We resolved to meet again as soon as Cindy could have the pictures developed.

That meeting in my living room several days later became another important step on the journey of my shifting worldview. When we examined the photos that Cindy had taken, we could all see, interwoven in the pictures, images of spirits, people, and alternate lifetimes. We felt awed, lifted up, and mesmerized. All three of us were able to see and witness what each of us discovered: the living room fell away into timelessness. We were moving through the pictures as if we were actually inside of them, but really there was no inside or outside anymore.

In one photo, when I looked into the background and at the configurations beyond the window, other images emerged: I could clearly see my Dad's life story depicted as if on film. He had been a Holocaust victim who was interred in a concentration camp. Now I could see him in the photo as a boy in hiding, crouched in the woods behind a clump of bushes on the left corner of the picture. I could see an SS man bending down over him. Behind, a scene of destruction was unfolding: there was smoke billowing everywhere. In front of it, over Sareeta's hand, my Dad was walking away from the destruction with a beer mug raised toward me in a toast. He wore a beach shirt and sunglasses and he looked younger, cheerful, and unperturbed. He chose to walk away.

I sat mesmerized, looking at that picture for who knows how long. What did it mean? It was like a visit from him. Did it mean he was ready to leave this world behind? Did he mean to tell me he was okay? The intensity of emotion between the two of us had often been enormously powerful, like white-water rapids: you know it is not wise to dabble in them unless you know how to maneuver in that current. But I had the distinct feeling that it was all there, alive, happening now or somewhere else in alternate lives. The holograph kept unfolding and showing me various sides of the universe.

Sareeta was deeply moved by something she saw in the photo Cindy had taken of her holding the picture of her brother. When we turned the photo sideways and studied the background, she could see Navin reclining with two children in his arms. He looked peaceful, content and at ease. As Sareeta pointed it out I saw it immediately and I sank into the picture with her, looking, absorbing the faint images which became clear as we focused on them. There was a division in the picture over Sareeta's left shoulder, and I studied the right side of it. What was I supposed to find? At first I couldn't see it, but knew something was there. Then I saw it. It was his skull, the base of the back of his skull, to be specific. Clear as a bell. How could I have missed it? The base of his skull showed two bruises, slightly more pronounced to the left—the very place where he had sustained injuries in the accident that claimed his life. Take a look at the photo here and see for yourself.

www.cindymay.com

I remembered how fascinating it was to look inside a kaleidoscope as a child. This deep seeing was even more wondrous, showing possibilities and realities upon realities. You could shift your gaze slightly and see something entirely different, a different reality playing out, another alternative.

When we became tired of time-traveling and ready to slip back into the safety of the living room, we felt a calm and excitement all in one. What happened that night sent a positive charge through each of us and further confirmed for me the power and depth of this new paradigm vision of reality.

All Happening Now: The Holograph

Through this profound experience with the timeless realities in the photographs, I finally really experientially understood how in the collective unconscious past, present, and future manifested simultaneously, with no distinguishable timeline. Different lives were all happening in front of our eyes, as our minds were freed from the boundaries of the boxes we live in on a day-to-day basis. It confirmed for me the importance of connecting to something much greater than our everyday existence. The material reality of my living room, for example, seemed insignificant in comparison. I found myself thinking, just a year ago I was fretting over the placement of a new decorative bowl. I was so dependent on the safety and familiarity of my bowl and my armchair! The security of the ordinary world is wonderful and I enjoy every moment of it, now even more than before, but there is so much we don't see, don't understand, and can't explain. I know what I saw that evening in those pictures. It was extraordinary, and it was real.

None of us will ever forget the exquisite freedom of that evening: my mind was expanded in its sense of possibilities, as if an inner eye had opened. With this new, expanded vision, I saw so much more than the familiar physical objects of my living room or the pictures of Sareeta. The real treasure, the real story, were the lives contained in those pictures. The connection between Navin and my Dad made sense to my conscious mind: they were both victims of interracial hate crimes. I knew that these discoveries would lead me to where I needed to go: I was finally beginning to trust the process.

A Channeled Message

Shortly after our session with the photographs, I found myself writing this message from Navin, whose words appeared to flow effortlessly from my pen.

A wish and good news from Navin.

Everybody loves spirit. You praise it, you want it, but many don't honor it. That's the truth. I'm not judging you, just observing you in action.

Looking in on humans from the outside makes it easy to be non-judgmental. You need to know this. You are where you are at every moment to understand that you are creating who you are.

Religions need to interface to combine their commonalities, their faith, rather than fight each other. Faith is a continuous process of creation in the image of the lightness of being. Every moment is an opportunity to be guided by spirit instead of the conditioned mind.

Find out what you are searching to gain for your spirit. To be successful, look at where you are now and look at long-term gains for your eternal soul, instead of short-term losses. This is a concept your mind will understand and your soul will prosper from. Most people believe in the dominance/submission game—looking for gains in their temporary material existence. That game is simply a blip in the lifetime of an ever-evolving universe.

This dominance/submission game led to what you call my death. The game is over for me, and I am glad. I chose not to participate at the moment I passed on. I chose to put myself above it. Now is my chance to touch you with my level of truth.

Thank you for the reception.

Yours truly,
Navin

Tarot and My Psychic Great-Grandmother

After my hand wrote this message from Navin, I ended the session in the tradition of my great-grandmother with a reading of tarot cards, using the Motherpeace deck which a friend gave me a long time ago. Whenever I play with the cards, I think of my mom's grandmother, the one my mother was named after. She had lost her husband in the First World War and was left to raise her children on her own, but she did this very ably because she had a natural gift of clairvoyance. Townspeople of all walks of life came to have their fortunes told.

That night, a card fell out of the deck for me and dropped on the floor: it was the Eight of Wands, which depicts flaming arrows shot from a bow held by a winged creature. According to the deck's creators, Vicki Noble and Karen Vogle, the card signifies messages, change, and inspiration, awakening the personality. It means taking a risk, trying something new, letting passions fly. It can also indicate the high energy of psychic power, allowing one to tune in on people's thoughts or wishes, "to hear the phone before it rings and know who's on the other end, to initiate a relationship that hasn't yet manifested on the physical plane." The appropriateness of this image made me feel very close to my great-grandmother.

Interestingly, I remembered that when I studied at the University of Toronto I rented a very large attic room in a huge old Victorian house. I loved that house and felt totally at home in my cozy attic room. It had a little triangular bay window which I loved nestling into. I had found an old handmade quilt with rose and rust colors which I spread over my large brass bed. When I described this room vividly to my mother, she seemed puzzled. "You are describing my grandmother's space, where she did her work," she told me. "She was not allowed to do that kind of work during WWII, so she had a trapdoor to an area off the attic where she could hide if there was a search. It was a risky business, but she had everybody in town as clients: the police, the mayor, and the soldiers. The officials could disappear behind the trapdoor, if they needed to. They must have trusted her and she trusted them because she was not arrested." Evidently, this great-grandmother had accurately predicted events during the Second World War.

Connecting with her was one of the steps toward owning my own gifts of seeing.

The Real Meaning of After-Death Messages

It cheers me that there are now programs on TV like *The Medium* and *Unsolved Mysteries*, showing us that crimes are often solved with the help of psychics who contact the victims on the other side: I take it as a sign that perhaps alternative ways of knowing are beginning to receive more respect. But the other side can also send a message of hope.

My story about Navin isn't about solving a murder; why or how he passed over seems less important than that his death have meaning. Navin's death does draw attention to the problems in Trinidad, but the real meaning of his communications transcends our understanding of life and death. He let me know that we need to see the higher order of things; it is crucial to him that something positive be ignited from his tragedy. Navin's family was undergoing relentless suffering. His mother, in particular, was devastated: she had no greater wish than to see her only son have children of his own. But now even she sees the situation with different eyes.

Navin's killer will have to stand his own trial, either in this life or the next; he will have to deal with his own misery eventually, and I have no desire or inclination to be a part of that. My task was to allow Navin to show us something about living and dying, and to point out the eternal nature of our souls.

What is most important about Navin's story? I believe it is the memory of his loving kindness that was so strong he was able to overcome death in order to bring comfort to his family. And he gave us important information about dying: he wants us to know that he did not suffer in the moment when he was lifted up and passed over, and that no one dies alone.

I believe that one way we can best serve his memory is to tell our own stories, to express ourselves, fueled by empathy for others. This is how we can heal. Navin's life needed to be given a voice. In hearing his story, and in telling our own, we are all healed.

It All Began with One Step

The most important step in my journey away from the old paradigm was my conscious decision to be more compassionate and empathic. As I became more compassionate, the world became a more loving, cooperative, open, and helpful place to me. It really is just that simple: becoming more compassionate ourselves allows us to receive the compassionate vibrations of our environment in return. It is pure bliss to surrender to the loving energies of the universe. It was from this place of transcendence and trust that I finally began to write the book I needed to write all along, the one you now hold. Every step on my journey brought me tremendously rewarding experiences, and it was the cumulative powerful, positive vibrations of those experiences that led to a true epiphany in my life.

My own personal epiphany arrived after a night when I had reached a level of empathy and compassion that made me feel totally complete. There was no more to do, nothing to accomplish, just to love like this, without judgment, to reach beyond all man-made boundaries and see the most profound truth the universe holds—that we are all one. I will share this transcendent experience with you in Part 3, but you need to know that it was an experience of ecstatic bliss, and—most importantly—that it is available to each of us.

So I invite you to continue on the journey with me, to witness more intriguing stories, and to see for yourself the healing benefits, both personal and global, offered by the new paradigm, the worldview of oneness, trust, and compassion.

PART 2

New Paradigm 101
What It Is and
How to Get There

"This shift therefore goes to the core of our lives. It is much more than a change in ideas and how we think. It is a change in our view of reality, identity, social relationships and human purpose. A paradigm shift can be felt in the body, heart, mind and soul."

—Duane Elgin, from *Promise Ahead: A Vision of Hope and Action for Humanity's Future*

This section of the book is designed to give you a crash course in New Paradigm thinking. It will explain some of its core principles, and introduce you to several of the great teachers, leaders, and healers in this movement toward a new way of being. It will also show you where you are right now, and offer practices to try that will help you to get from here to there.

First, the word "paradigm" itself has only come into common usage recently. It was Thomas Kuhn, a scientist and professor of the history of science, who first made the term popular in the early '60s. In Kuhn's view, a paradigm is not simply the current theory, *but the entire world view in which it exists*, and all of the implications which come with it. He was talking about science, but now it is applied to many aspects of life. So, within a worldview, we have attitudes, beliefs, thoughts, images, and rules about how the world works.

Paradigms shift when it gradually becomes clear that the current paradigm doesn't explain everything that is happening. For instance, for millennia the world was believed to be flat as a pancake. Then scientific discoveries proved otherwise, but it took a very long while before most people were fully convinced that the world was round. In fact, this paradigm shift created a storm of controversy, much as Darwin's theory of evolution, or the discovery of dinosaur bones, did hundreds of years later. Keep in mind that the system itself is usually very slow to change. But when it becomes apparent that there are factors at work that don't fit the current paradigm, a state of crisis evolves. During this crisis, new ideas, perhaps ones previously discarded, are tried. Eventually a *new* paradigm is formed, which gains its own new followers. We are in that crisis time now. Global warming, tsunamis, and raging religious wars are calling us to wake up and pay attention. It is time to end the old story and begin a new one.

It was the journey toward fully embracing my sensitivity that revealed a way into the emerging paradigm to me. It is a journey that each of us can take. The benefits are an expanded sense of what is possible, and a life of abundance, passion, and purpose.

The Paradigm Quiz

Before we can do any shifting, though, we need to know where we are right now. It is always a clarifying process to take a good hard look at our beliefs, so here is a fun and easy way for you to do that. Where are you in on the paradigm scale? You can give this quiz to your friends and family to see where they fit in, as well.

Decide—as honestly as you can—which statement of each pair most closely sums up your belief about each numbered issue.

1. The nature of reality
   a. Reality is only what can be proven. It is concrete, ordinary, measurable, and objective.
   b. Reality is subjective and objective reality is an illusion. Reality can be extra-ordinary and essentially mysterious.

2. The power of humans
   a. We only affect ourselves. Individual actions have no consequences on Humans as a species. Thoughts have no influence because they cannot be seen.
   b. We have access to the collective database. The universe is participatory. We, as humans, participate in co-creation with the universe with our thoughts, actions and intentions.

3. Energy
   a. We use our energy to create our personal empire. The bigger the empire, the greater the individual.
   b. Energy is all around us. The universe is alive, conscious, intelligent and compassionate. The more we tap into that, the more energy we have.

4. Consciousness
   a. Humans are the only life form with consciousness.
   b. All life forms have consciousness.

5. Universe
   a. The earth is the only place where intelligent life resides. The earth is the center of the universe.
   b. The universe is a seamless web of interconnections. The earth is at the heart of that splendid, gigantic, holographic web.

Key: Obviously, the more "b" answers you chose, the closer you are to living the New Paradigm. But even if you chose several Old Paradigm answers, remember that it is the desire to change that powers the change. And if we focus on being angry at ourselves or others for being stuck in the Old Paradigm, that just keeps us stuck in it! As we gradually apply more new thoughts and images to our lives, we shift more fully into a new way of living.

Building the Pyramids

Here is an easy way to understand the basic core beliefs, the ground-rules, if you will, of both Old and New Paradigms.

A pyramid—that ancient structure so tied to the concept of sacred geometry (more about that later)—is the perfect shape to house the code of living we need to embrace in order to open ourselves and learn to be powered by intention.

First, though, we need to look at the pyramid structure created by the current paradigm:

The Fear Pyramid

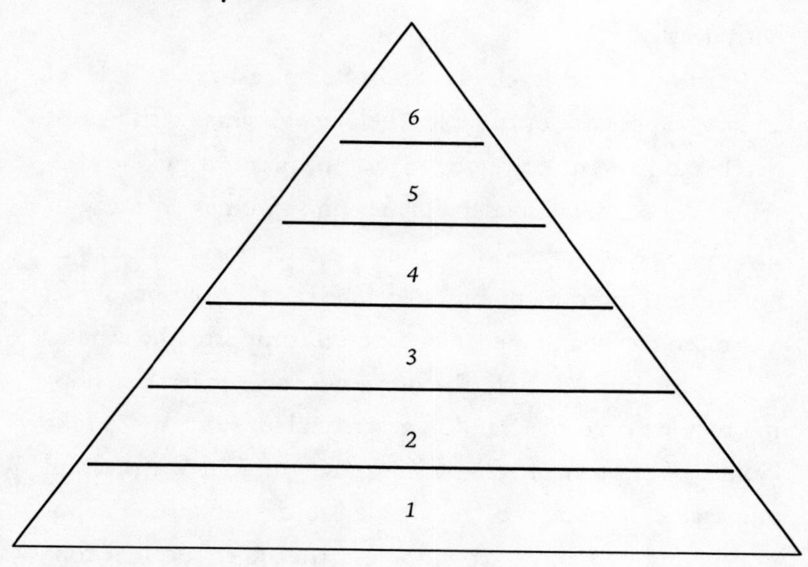

1. Fear of death.
2. Fear based on perceived wrongs. Perception of oneself as a victim.
3. A need to be in control permeates, resolved by angry reactions.
4. Defensive reactions and suspicion.
5. This we solve by competition, a more sophisticated solution than violence.
6. Not having enough. This is the highest rung we have created so far.

The first level in this pyramid is a place of struggle with the fear of death. All layers built on that foundation reflect this hopelessness. We fear that life will be taken away from us, so we may as well pack in all the hedonism we can. In fact, many of us avoid thinking about death until it is actually upon us. Life is conducted in a firm denial of a relationship with death.

On the second level, our desire for pleasure is hindered and we experience ourselves as helpless victims, with fear of death, pain and negative power (Satan) permeating our existence. We see sadness, dependency and traumas as a way of life. We often react to this with apathy, depression, and anxiety and feel there are no real solutions to this dilemma of life. We often feel abandoned, alone, and unsupported by others.

On the third level, we give our power over to leaders, hoping they will "fix" the fear. On a personal level, we try to take control of our fear, often by feeling angry instead of afraid and vulnerable. We start to feel entitled to do something about our victimhood and start acting out the anger through control over others. This is the destructive expression of greed and entitlement. Pride, self-righteous behavior, and fanaticism are fueled by that anger.

On the fourth level, we become aware of the anger and fear all around us and we are suspicious. When is the next shoe going to drop? When are we going to become the victim? Our bodies and minds are in alarm states most of the time. Adrenalin-driven fight-or-flight reactions are the norm. Being the bully is perceived as the preferred way of being. "Who wants to be the victim?" we ask. We display faulty attachment behaviors, expressed in a defensive, numbing and distancing way of relating to one another.

On level five, we resolve to be competitive. This is a more sophisticated way of dealing with fear and anger. Through the power of reason we transcend the rage of hot-headed anger and the sadness of despair. We learn to handle our personality self in such a way that we are capable of exerting influence and manipulating outcomes to gain from them. We grow our empire only to discover it is...

... never enough. The sixth level. We feel we will never have enough money, power, or convenience in our life. After all, life is finite and it will soon be taken away. There is never enough time to enjoy all this, or enough security to feel really content and relaxed. Children aren't accomplished enough, parents aren't cool enough, a wife is not young enough anymore, or our country isn't powerful enough. The highest rung in this pyramid is all about scarcity.

The Freedom Pyramid

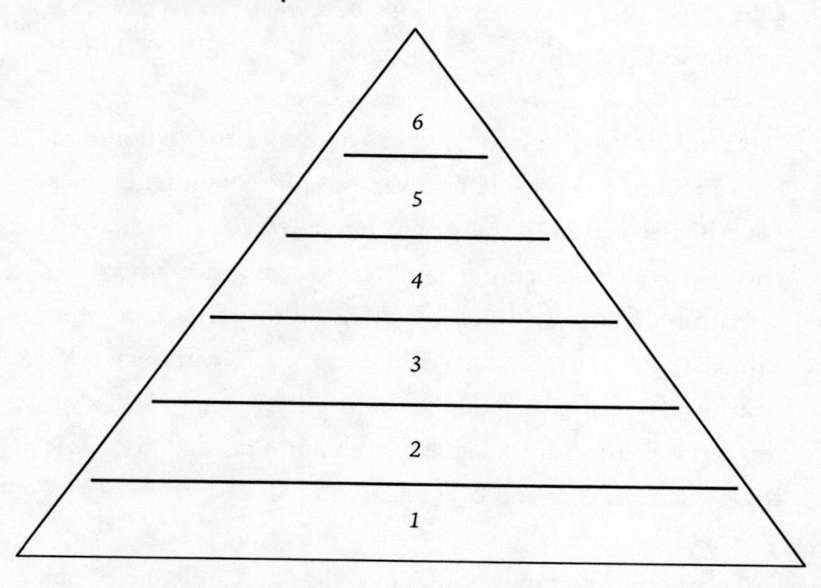

1. Divine Purpose (awareness of infinite Spirit and the connectedness of all).
2. Learning (the meaning of experience).
3. Letting go (trusting and giving over to the Mystery).

4. Synchronicity and power of intention in action.
5. Win/Win (What goes around comes around, open to creating abundance).
6. Abundance (letting the universe show the Divine Proportions).

The first level—the foundation—is always the most important, since it affects how solid the structure will be. The foundation of the Freedom Pyramid is the recognition of our essential love and divinity. It is like the Great Pyramid, based on the universal measurement of perfection in the phi principle. This is the foundation which holds the secret to life. Our spirit lives whether our body decays or not. We build a relationship with life in concordance with a relationship to death.

From the second level springs the desire to learn and to find out more about what makes the universe tick. It fuels your higher learning, the desire for knowledge. The difference between advancing in our purpose and not advancing is learning from our mistakes. Making mistakes is a good thing. It shows that we take risks and are active in the world. Learning from our mistakes is the application of knowledge: it is our ticket to advancing to a level of not needing to repeat these mistakes over and over again.

The third level is the experience of freedom and real control over our direction in life. We realize we can let go of old patterns, of repeating the same lessons. We realize we can substitute old patterns with new, more productive ones. As we grow new connections based on our observation of how we and the environment dance together very intimately, we become increasingly aware of our sixth sense. We are then able to integrate our multi-sensory nature. We develop a patient confidence which allows for divine timing rather than the pure force of will.

On the fourth level, we observe the synchronicity fueled by the power of intention. Learning becomes accelerated and we understand and accept the power of intuition. We are open to guidance beyond linear thought.

On the fifth level, we are applying the principles of win/win. There is an expansive power in creating cooperative solutions in all our relationships. Efforts fueled by concern for others come back to us multifold. Our life is becoming more and more expansive and as we cooperate the universe cooperates with us. We are in the natural flow of life, opening to love and beauty.

Level six is where the gift of life is realized fully by recognizing the abundant nature of the universe. There is joy in both the ordinary and the extraordinary, which is felt as an expression of love and divinity. There is a desire to tap into this creative power for the benefit of all, rather than for personal gain. Limits are perceived as impositions created by outdated belief systems.

Living the Freedom Pyramid

It is amazing to think that as long ago as 3000 years, the ancient Egyptians drew upon sophisticated knowledge of mathematical formulae relating to angles, heights and distances, and made detailed maps of places and of the stars in the sky. The foundation of the Great Pyramid at Giza, built for King Khufu around 2800 BCE, rested on this knowledge. Now, in the continuum of human evolution, instead of being called to create vast monuments to dead rulers, we are being asked to build our House of Eternity together. Although we have internalized the old Fear Pyramid, the new millennium is the perfect time for us to undertake the work of shifting human consciousness.

Choosing to live in the Freedom Pyramid doesn't mean that we don't feel any of the levels of the Fear Pyramid. It is human to feel fear, anger, or a need for control, to struggle with those feelings, and to learn from them. But when we see our feelings from the foundation of the Freedom Pyramid—from a sense of the immortality of our spirits—then it puts our emotions in the proper perspective, and they can transform into something more positive and empowering. For example, instead of acting out of rage, we can look at our feelings of anger with compassion, saying "My rage is telling me something important. What does it have to teach me? How is it my ally? It is good to remember that I do not have to feel this way." The Freedom Pyramid is ultimately about co-operation, collaboration, and teaching each other.

When we superimpose the foundation of infinity over the lowest rung on the Fear Pyramid we notice a transition taking place. It becomes a holograph reflecting both realities, changing as our perspective changes. The Fear Pyramid then becomes a true pyramid, holding in its center the sacred geometry which infuses it with light.

The Magic Equation

How can we change mass consciousness so that humanity can reach a positive tipping point? This simple formula, which I received in a powerful spiritual guidance dream, tells us how:

$$P = M \times E$$

Believe me, I am not a mathematical thinker, so this dream was a surprise to me. Here is the meaning I received about it:

Power = Mass times Energy. Mass means the mass of people, the masses. The more people involved, the more power achieved. The energy (E) is the vibrational level of the person. It is the spirit with which the masses are affected. This can happen on an everyday level: for instance, a baker affects the masses (M) by the way he smiles when selling bread. This in turn affects the power (P) of the collective database for all humanity. The school bus driver's energy has an impact by the way he receives the children. Love spreads love.

It is known now that everything has a vibration; even objects which seem inert and motionless are swirling with energy. Many believe that feelings have vibrations, too, and that like vibrations attract more of the same. For instance, when we feel love and trust, this adjusts our personal energy field to receive more loving, trusting feelings and experiences. It is also thought that the vibrational levels of love and trust are higher than those of prejudice and fear. When the masses catch on to that, the Power (P) available to humanity becomes positively charged.

We affect each other hugely in our daily lives. It is in just this way that we will create the New Paradigm: our behaviors and beliefs can create enough Mass on a higher vibrational level to create Power from positive Energy, rather than from violence and destruction.

The Network: Science, Interconnectedness, and Holographs

Recently, Dr. Alain Aspect, a physicist at the University of Paris, made a discovery that may change the face of science. He and his research team found that subatomic particles such as electrons are able to instantaneously communicate with each other regardless of the distance separating them. It doesn't matter whether they are 3 feet or 3 billion miles apart; somehow each particle always seems to know what the other is doing.

Ancient Wise Ones have always known that all things in the universe are connected. Consider this beautiful passage from the sacred Hindu Vedas, over 7000 years old:

There is an endless net of threads throughout the Universe.
The horizontal threads are in space: the vertical threads in time:
At every crossing of threads there is an individual, and
every individual is a pearl.
The great light of Absolute Being illuminates and penetrates
every pearl.
And also, every pearl reflects not only the light from every
other pearl in the net,
But also every reflection of every reflection throughout the
Universe.

Perhaps science is finally beginning to catch up to ancient wisdom. According to Michael Talbot in his book *The Holographic Universe*, if a hologram of a rose is cut in half and then illuminated by a laser, each half still contains the entire image of the rose. If you keep dividing the halves, each snippet of film again contains a smaller but intact version of the original image. Every part of a hologram contains all the information of the whole. If we apply this to the universe, then it is a superhologram, which contains "All that Is."

Michael Talbot states that the electrons in a carbon atom in the human brain are connected to the subatomic particles that comprise every salmon that swims, every heart that beats, and every star that shimmers in the sky. In other words, energy from the tapestry of the entire universe is present in every person and any form of matter—the energy being in fact part of a whole, instead of being mistakenly perceived as a separate entity. The "whole in every part" nature of a hologram provides us with an entirely new way of understanding the organization and order of the universe. This new model of reality says that individual brains access portion of the network—the greater hologram where everything is infinitely interconnected. This can be an explanation for how telepathy works.

Much has been written about the 100th monkey principle: scientists observed that monkeys on an island learned a complex new task by watching their leader. Only those that watched could perform the task, while the other monkeys could not. Meanwhile, in a completely different part of the world, monkeys suddenly began doing the same task. This is a perfect example of the collective subconscious, when we just suddenly know something, pick it up out of "nowhere," because we are connected to the network.

Science and spirituality are finally beginning to agree on this vision of connection. Physicists increasingly describe the Universe as a single, dynamically-interconnected cosmic web, in which the whole determines the actions of its parts and the parts the whole. This was the Universe envisioned by Eastern mystics or seers, thousands of years ago. In Buddhism it is described as Dharmakaya, the Body of Being. In Taoism it is the Tao, meaning the Whole, the One Thing, the Way or the Cosmic Process. In Hinduism it is Brahman, which means That Which Expands.

Sacred Geometry

Sacred Geometry offers a vision of harmony and beauty if we know how to look. When I received the Greek letter *phi* in a dream, it led me to a study of the Golden Ratio. I found out that we are literally surrounded by divine proportions. The Golden Ratio is also known as the Divine Proportion and it is found in any number of nature's structures, as well as in architecture and art. The ratio of length to width is approximately 1.618 and is seen as most visually pleasing, holding the divine harmony of human nature within. The human face shows the *phi* ratio: top models' faces conform more closely to the *phi* ratio than those of average people. If you divide the pitch of a DNA spiral by its diameter you get the Golden Ratio. In nature the Divine Proportion shows up everywhere: for example the lengths of the sections of the butterfly form *phi* ratios, the length and width of the wings, the size of the head compared to its width and length, and so on and on. When we recognize the presence of true beauty around us, we realize that we are surrounded by divine harmony.

In a powerful precognitive dream about my father's death, I received the distinct vision of a spiral. Researching this shape led me to see its fundamental presence in nature: the

Golden Mean spiral is everywhere. We are living in a spiral galaxy, we hear sounds using the little spiral apparatus in our ears. There are spirals in pinecones, seashells, sunflowers and countless other plants. Clearly, it is another symbol of geometry expressing the Divine in the ordinary. And according to Pamela Ball's dream book, the spiral is the ideal path to growth and evolution. Everything is continually in motion, but also continually rising or raising its vibration. A clockwise spiral, moving outward to the right, is a movement towards consciousness and enlightenment. When I dreamed my father's death, the spiral I saw was moving in exactly this way.

These symbols and forms are prevalent in works of art as well. Most people know Leonardo's famous drawing of the Vitruvian Man: it is the most recognizable image he created and has been used as a symbol of human inspiration by many teachers of spiritual and universal wisdom. Leonardo was fascinated with patterns; the spiraling motifs we see in many of his paintings show his interest in the helix form, just like the helix of the DNA holding each individual's genetic code. Leonardo integrated ancient geometry and the Golden Ratio in many of his paintings, giving visual expression to the truths that unite rather than divide us.

The ancient Greeks and the Egyptians truly understood the *phi* ratio: although the Greek Parthenon and the Great Pyramid look very different from one another, both integrate the mathematical formula of the Golden Ratio. In the emerging paradigm we integrate both sides of the brain, just as the ancient Greeks and Egyptians did when they created a piece of art. The left brain was used to measure everything carefully and to make sure it was mathematically correct according to the *phi* proportion. The right brain was used to optimize creativity. If our left brains can understand and utilize these mathematics, it enhances rather than hinders our creative process. Absorbing the spiritual significance of sacred geometry is one path to transformation. Simple contemplation of the pinecone or the sunflower can bring us to an altered state of consciousness, a knowing of the mysterious depth of the universe, and the realization that all of nature is divinely proportioned, divinely ordered.

Recently, seeing the beautifully vibrant red tulips in full bloom at the entrance of a library, I remembered that I used to draw these exact tulips when I was a child about ten years old. They had pointy edges, opening out at a perfect angle, and bright red petals with yellow divisions. I remember drawing these tulips over and over again to get them perfect; doing so gave me great peace. I also remember asking myself, Why this particular painting? I think I know now. It was about my own inner discovery of the *phi* ratio as described here. It was my own inner pyramid in the making, the one built on infinity, learning and the Divine Proportion. What shapes give you a feeling of harmony, balance, and inner peace? Do you resonate with circle or squares, triangles or spirals? Our preference for certain shapes can tell us something about our own inner natures. Those who prefer squares, for instance, may be innately drawn to order and safety. Circle-folks are egalitarian and pursue wholeness. People who resonate with triangles aspire upwards but remain grounded, and spiral-lovers have a deep understanding of the repeating patterns of our lives.

Making the Shift

"The most powerful thing you can do to change the world, is to change your own beliefs about the nature of life, people, reality, to something more positive and begin to act accordingly..."

—Shakti Gawain

What we see depends on our point of view, our perception. As Gary Zukav says, "Without perception, the Universe continues...to generate an endless profusion of possibility. With perception, however, all the possibilities collapse, except one part, which actualizes into reality."

There are endless possibilities existing as energy forms and electromagnetic forces are everywhere. But when we focus on or become aware of one of these possibilities, it becomes real to us and the others cease to exist in our perception. In fact electromagnetic forces are the most prevalent force in the universe. Science has shown that, in order to attract a force we want, we need to be in alignment with it, otherwise, we will actually repel it, rather than attracting it.

As humans, the greatest rewards come from creating a strong emotional field which attracts our desired energies. The freedom pyramid I've described is such a place for nourishing the soul and aligning ourselves with the energies we want to attract. At any point, we have infinite possibilities to choose from, but it is our own perspective that really does the choosing of energy forms. The Paradigm quiz and the Freedom and Fear pyramids can help you to become aware of which paradigm you are choosing for yourself at a particular time. Your choices are bound to be very different when you start integrating the many new paradigm principles outlined in this book. These principles are aligned with the forces to attract love, abundance, and peace.

Knowing this, I have been imagining that there is a place beyond fear, beyond polarized consciousness, beyond power-over, where we live in joy as Essence. More and more of us are realizing the power, the wonder, and the peace we experience when we get into the "zone" of shifting paradigms. More and more of us realize how we thrive in this positively charged energy and how this affects all of humanity. In Part 3, I will give more real life examples of new paradigm living, as well as practices that can help you to expand your energies in the field of empathy, sensitivity and intuition that lead to manifesting our truest inner desires.

Why hasn't anyone ever told you this before? Well, many have tried, but we need many more people to go forth with conviction to be able to teach others. For this to occur, more and more empathic people need to become leaders in this world. Taking a new look at the world, and seeing it differently, is certainly an important step towards bringing in the new way of being and behaving in the world. But we need to see ourselves differently, as well.

The following section deals with some of the steps we can take as individuals to help bring about the change. Here they are in brief.

1. **Break out of Old Paradigm roles.** Part of the journey toward the New Paradigm is becoming aware of all the masks we wear—the personality roles we play—and how they im-

prison us. Many people play roles and games and think that is who they are. In fact, far from it. It is when we are able to see the roles we play and masks we wear that we can free ourselves from them and change our future.

2. **Own our shadow selves.** When we play roles, we develop "holes" in our personalities, and disown those parts of us: these are the parts we deem undesirable in society. When we look compassionately at the disowned parts of ourselves (and there is an easy way to find out what those are), we become more integrated and whole as humans, and it is easier to be compassionate toward others. Taking responsibility for our emotions, accepting them, and looking to them for information rather than repressing them or acting out in harmful ways is also an important part of this step.

3. **Relate differently to the concepts of good and evil.** When we accept that each of us has the capacity for good or evil within us, and that we have true freedom, we can begin to see the range of possibilities for positive choices.

4. **Claim our Empathic power.** Owning our gifts as compassionate empaths, and behaving more in accordance with them, is truly the key to changing the pattern of humanity.

Steps on the Journey to Freedom

My wish for all sensitive people is to let go of their shyness and hiding by stepping into their power—to let their spirits shine and their hearts sing out loud.

These guidelines are designed to help sensitive intuitive empaths step into more powerful roles in society.

1. Breaking Out of Old Paradigm Roles: Bullies and Victims

What Old Paradigm roles do we play? Many of us are caught in victim or bully behavior, but these roles are based on the old fearful way of being, from a sense of separateness rather than unity or connection.

Shifting out of these old roles involves a willingness to embrace new ways of looking at the world and how we can thrive much better as a human race. In order to evolve constructively, we need to adjust our stagnant patterns in six fundamental ways. We need to change:

1. our ways of knowing
2. our beliefs
3. our heart
4. our attitudes
5. our behaviors

All these shifts will result in

6. a change in our biology

In the last decade, scientists are realizing that the human brain can be "rewired." We can change our behaviors and, ultimately, our biology when we live in a more constructive energy frequency. But for this to occur, more sensitive, intuitive, and feeling people must step up to the plate and lead the way. To passively sit back is depriving humanity of the benefits empathy can bring to us all.

As we play old paradigm roles as if they are reality, we continue to strengthen and create that reality. We are only as good as the limitations we play out. These roles are based on the control structure which permeates our ego-driven society.

The ego is the part in us that thinks it knows how we *should* be, based on our interpretation of the messages we got from our family, teachers, and society in general. Just as the physical body develops from baby to child to adult, we develop an ego over time—and this is a necessary stage.

Since we listen to the ego a lot, we often forget we are much more than our personality self, that we are spirit, our belief systems, our learned paradigm, all of it. From the limited personality perspective everything is seen in terms of power—who has power and who doesn't. And in terms of competition—Who wins? Who loses? The ego is always hungry, seeking more and more—money, love, food, sex, power.

When you are playing a game of dominance and submission, your interpretation of an event has gone rigid. You see things from the way you think they "should" be from your limited perspective, where you either play the victim ("somebody did this to me") and feel sorry for yourself, or you feel entitled to retaliate, one stance often following the other. We can alleviate this rigidity by letting go of our black-or-white vision that is really a blind spot. If you can peek out from behind the blind spot and see around the corner to how the other person perceives the situation or how she feels, you can truly see again. If we allow playfulness to enter and don't take ourselves too seriously, we are often able to extend the olive branch.

Recently, I had a client who is a self-proclaimed bully. He told me he wanted to stop shouting, using foul language, and intimidating others with his size. His wife had given him an ultimatum and he seriously wanted to change his anger patterns. In our session, he discovered that he turned into a bully at five years old. His reaction to how he saw the world was to be angry, defensive, and ready to fight. As a young boy he had made a decision not to be the victim (he saw his mother that way), but to defend himself. He had a bully as a father and he did not feel safe around him. In the session, he realized this five-year-old deserved to be safe and he deserved to want love. From that perspective, he could provide the love this five year old needed for himself as an adult. He can now be the positive father for himself that he always wanted. He cried for a long time out of relief over being able to allow himself the feeling of wanting love. Then he cried over the time when he was eight and he had hurt a girl he liked. He hurt her because that was the only thing he could think of to do so that he could then help her, be her rescuer which, he thought, would make her like him. It dawned on him during the session that it would have been much easier to just talk to her.

Bullies have difficulty admitting that they too are motivated by the desire to be loved. Instead, they attempt to gain the esteem of friends through "faulty attachment" behavior, like embarrassing somebody in front of the person they want to be liked by. This, they reason, should create a bond with the desired person. Or they do what my client did and hurt somebody to be able to rescue them later.

It is difficult for bullies to be attached. They may have had parents who used control as attachment behaviors, which made for rather inconsistent attachment. Having an inconsistent ability to attach is like having an internal thermometer which keeps them at a certain level of comfort from the love they get. If they are not used to much love, their internal love-thermometer is set rather low, let's say at 65 degrees. Every time there is too much love coming their way, the heat goes up to an uncomfortable level, for example 74 degrees. This is too much—they're not used to it—so they might pick a fight and their internal thermometer adjusts to keeping them somewhere around 63 to 67 degrees. What they need to do is to go outside their comfort zone to be able to set their love-thermometer higher. Then they will be able to take in the love they want.

Each of us has the potential for being a victim and a bully. Both of these are roles that the ego/personality plays based on the rules and the conditions of the old paradigm, playing out and keeping our fears alive.

Both the victim and the bully see themselves as lonely and wronged. The victim may be sensitive, but has tuned into a level of fear. Victims have bought into the dominance-submission game and feel powerless. They believe life is out to get them and there is nothing they can do to change it. They give up or collapse when they are stressed. The reality that plays out for them is one of learned helplessness, reinforced by media messages and intimidation by those who dominate. Images that keep that paradigm alive and create anxiety are in the best interests of the companies that want to sell us food, pills, clothes, and cosmetic surgery to make us feel better. Keeping us anxious serves the industries we have established.

The bully is on that same dominance/submission continuum of learned helplessness, but he has decided it is better to be on the side of the aggressor, to feel more powerful. Learned helplessness of either type can be unlearned if we change our paradigms.

We've all seen couples caught in power struggles believing they have to teach each other lessons: the old "I-know-better-than-you-do" attitude. This is based on fears—of losing control, of getting hurt—and ultimately it can feel like a life and death struggle. Out of fear, they feel they need to protect themselves and can shut each other down. With practice, though, this can shift so that they can see that the real question is, "What is the lesson here?" We learn to honor the other's struggles as much as our own.

Honoring the other does not mean being a doormat, though—far from it. The doormat is the victim. She later believes she is entitled to retaliate. Instead, she needs to close the door to abusive behavior, detaching her energy from that behavior and not giving up her power to it. The abused person—and more often it is the woman—needs to set her boundaries. There can be no tolerance for invasion, and she needs to feel her own energy, her joy, her conviction for what she stands for. It is like invaders entering a country during war: if there are enough resistance fighters, the invasion will be unsuccessful. This is why I admire women like Oprah so much: she takes a clear stand and inspires and encourages women to create that critical mass, which we can only do if there is a movement.

It is important to state here that, if you are in actual physical danger from your mate, you must protect yourself by accepting the help of a shelter or agency designed to understand and deal with the danger you face. Being a doormat is not a solution. You owe it to yourself to seek protection.

However, apart from situations of real physical violence, you can create safety in your home with compassion. If both of you can arrive at a point of empathy for each other, you are back on track with creating the marriage you can have. You can then let go of blaming the other person for their earlier blind spot. The content usually isn't important at all. It takes more work for the self-righteous ones to come out of that stance. They see themselves as so lonely and so wronged. Every brain cell is firing confirmation for the events that occurred to justify this feeling. The cycle continues. In reality the brain cells are just doing what they are used to. We have created a neuro-network that confuses the excitement of these power struggles with love. We have to create new synapses, new network connections, in the human database.

In my own marriage, we still occasionally play our ego roles and we know what happens when each of us feels unloved and hurt by the other. We start out with feeling like the victim, and then feel entitled to hurt the other and thus become the bully. Neither of us wants to give in and we certainly don't want to hear the other person's accusations.

To shift this, I tune into loving my husband again, by seeing his pain, rather than his bullying. So I say something kind, despite my still-bruised ego, give a smile and a touch, and slow myself down. We have a choice: whether to be self-righteous or happy. Happiness comes from a loving state where we are assertive instead of abusive. We have learned that we can go beyond the meltdowns and the power struggles. We still go there sometimes, but we go back to seeing our true motivation: to love and be loved. Our database, based on old patterns, is changing; our power struggles are becoming less frequent and our ability to choose joy and happiness is increasing. On the other hand, power struggles do serve a purpose: through them, we get to know our negative sides, to become familiar with them, and to choose what we really want in life.

Our reality depends on our interpretation, which depends on our perspective—like the example of one fish in its bowl observed from two different angles by two cameras. The results, projected on two different television screens, are ambiguous and can be misleading. Are we looking at two different fish or the same one? Ultimately, we can decide to believe whatever we want. We can shift our perspective.

In Sylvia Browne's book, *The Nature of Good and Evil,* she says that we are all actually away from Home and our experiences here on earth are a kind of "Boot Camp." We're going to learn a lot of skills, and once we get those, we're going back Home and staying there. I like the idea that earth is a schoolroom and we are here to learn lessons. It helps to shift any pain I may be experiencing—it gives it positive meaning.

Another way to make a shift is to consider the nature of our true relationship to the planet. Here is what Dr. David Suzuki, Canadian biologist and environmentalist, says about this:

We are all breathing the same air. We are all taking in the same atoms, and through these atoms we are connected to all living creatures in our surroundings and in the world, and to the past and the future. As it's the same with water. Our bodies are more than 60% water by weight. Water connects us all over the planet. What we do to water is what we do to us. Soil is what keeps us alive. We are the earth because most of the food we eat comes from the earth - we absorb it and make it into our body. Then we return to earth. We are also fire. Plants capture sunlight and convert the energy into sugar to give our bodies fuel. We are born from nature and are one with nature.

[David Suzuki, *Documentary: Suzuki Speaks*]

As human beings, we have been the bully in relationship to the Earth. It is not too late to take care of nature if we wake up, if we shift our perspective so that we learn to wonder, to watch the magic of the real world instead of indulging in the fragmentation game we have learned to play based on our mantra: "Economics is the centre of humanity." We are made up of atoms, and they don't disappear when we die. We return to the earth and we become a part of what is our home. There is no separation between ourselves and the planet.

Our thoughts and actions have a profound impact on the environment. In experiments on how our thoughts affect water, conducted by Dr. Masuro Emoto and shown in the movie, *What the Bleep Do We Know?*, it is possible to see how the structure of water cells changes depending on the thoughts we send to them. The ones given messages of love look like sparkling snowflakes—they are beautiful in shape and very light. The ones that have hate or anger sent to them are misshapen and dark.

Dr. Spencer Nadler, a surgical pathologist for over 25 years, echoes this idea in his book, *The Language of Cells*. He describes brain cells observed under a microscope, this way: in healthy brain cells, the ducts and lobules look like "hydrangeas, ponds, and rivers floating serenely." Damaged cells look like "distorted hula hoops."

It makes us wonder about the thoughts we have for others. Perhaps we should think again, before calling them "stupid" or "ugly" in our minds. If thoughts can have that affect on water, what about people? After all, we are mostly water.

We are our spirit, we are water, we are what we eat that comes from the earth—all of it is in us. We are profoundly connected with everything that is. We are love. We are evolving human beings...

2. Owning Our Shadow Selves

We play many roles besides the victim or the bully on a daily basis. The very important person, the complainer, or the nice girl are all examples of roles we take on to help ourselves cope in society. They are social masks, where we pretend to be better, weaker, tougher, or more polite than we actually feel.

These roles are useful in helping us cope—and there is nothing wrong with that; we do live in this world and we need to cope. But when we are stuck in certain roles and emotions that don't serve us, we are held back from being all that we can be. For example, as Empaths we prefer not to offend anybody. Because we aim to please others, we disown the parts of ourselves that we think are not pleasing—so owning those parts of ourselves which could rock the boat is a departure from our comfort zone. We are far more likely to see ourselves as the cause of anger, rather than recognizing that we are angry ourselves. However, it is crucially important for more compassionate and spirited people to take a leading role.

There are two steps to becoming aware of the disowned parts of ourselves.

1. Notice when we get triggered but something someone has said or done—when we get worked up, and have an emotional reaction of discomfort, anger, distrust or anxiety. For instance, we may be triggered by others' angry outbursts. We need to watch how this relates to us, in order to gain an understanding of our own issues. We may be holding in our anger and it comes out intermittently after long, bottled-up periods. Often, we decide to deal with conflict in this way because it worked in the environment in which we grew up, but now it is actually hurting us. We need to find the angry one in ourselves, be responsible for it and learn to handle the consequences. For an insightful and concise guide that shows how to turn anger into a constructive force, I've found Dr. Harriet Goldhor Lerner's *The Dance of Anger* very helpful. The book helps define boundaries and explains how to find true assertiveness instead of vacillating between being "nice" or "bitchy."

2. Notice when we have feelings of wanting to be like someone, believing that we are not. For example, we may meet someone who is very wealthy and notice we feel poor and unhappy. In this case, our disowned part is the wannabe-wealthy one inside us. We experience money as being out there, but we don't get the lucky breaks. Before we can develop the belief systems necessary to obtain wealth—or to actively choose otherwise—first we need to own part of us

that wants to be wealthy. Only if a part of us wants to be wealthy will we be triggered.

Here is a great way to own your shadow stuff, or your disowned parts: play them out. It's surprisingly fun. When I was in training to be a Gestalt therapist, we did an exercise that taught me a lot. We started with the premise that each of us has a main persona that helps us function in life. We all had perfected the parts we wanted others to see. In my group, for example, there was the intellectual doctor, the nice social worker, and the angry poet. During this exercise, we had to identify the parts in each other's personalities that we would feel most uncomfortable with. For example, the intellectual doctor would be very uncomfortable in the role of the village idiot. He hated to feel stupid. The angry poet would have to act out his least favorite role: the conformant to society's rules. The nice social worker could never be angry; it just wasn't in her repertoire, she was too kind for that. She was told her role would be the angry trouble maker. Then we had to pair up and spend half a day in society with our disowned parts in attendance.

My peers had observed I was withholding physical contact. So I became a person who loves hugging others. And I got to be seductive: not having physical contact was a way to hold my sexuality in tight check. I had a blast walking up to people and being up-close and personal, something I realized I had sorely neglected. Since then, it has actually become a much-cherished part of my personality. I discovered that we make decisions at one point and then forget that we have made them or that we can change them when they don't suit us anymore! I decided I was missing out on a lot of fun and I could revise my choices.

Our nice social worker went to Kensington Market and was thrown out by an irate vegetable merchant: she had unleashed so much pent up emotion that she actually became abusive. As it turned out, after the initial torrent of anger, she found her control over her anger and when or when not to employ it. Within a couple of months her lifetime acne problem had cleared up and her relationship with her husband had reached a new level of respect. She wasn't going to be pushed around anymore. She now owned her forceful side playfully and was in control of it, instead of it controlling her.

And the intellectual doctor? He was a wonderful village idiot. His pants were hiked up to just below his chest, his shirt threadbare, and he wore suspenders. His expression was baffled and he had no answers. He had a lot of fun letting his guard down and he thoroughly enjoyed not being "on" all the time. Before this experience he was very aloof and proud of his educated status. Afterwards, he was just as educated, but he became human and approachable, and I'm sure his bedside manner improved greatly.

The angry poet had a hard time identifying with the structured side of himself. He too learned the benefits of control he gained by accepting responsibility. He realized "just open the envelope and actually do the banking" had many rewards. After all, his responsibilities would not disappear whether he ignored them or not; the inner voices would just become more insistent. So, he decided to attend to them.

Reclaiming our disowned parts frees us from much pent-up emotion and we realize how much richer our lives are when we can access and express these emotions. For instance, owning anger can show us how kind we actually are, and how principled. We can learn how not to be afraid of our anger, how to express it, how we can let it move through us and let go of it. Anger can even fuel our successes if channeled productively, without cruelty and disrespect. For example, when we persevere, when we excel in adversity, we don't allow ourselves to give up. We are fighters, survivors and risk takers. We use the adrenaline anger gives us to act in spite of fear. When we can include healthy anger in our repertoire we can learn the language of assertiveness.

Suppressing that energy and sitting on it calls for a release—a celebration of letting it go. Owning disowned parts doesn't mean we will stay in that role, but it does give us a choice, and often we realize that we are not like that after all—or maybe only just a bit. When that bit irks us, we can laugh at it and let it go. Or we can use it, if it serves us well. For instance, I now feel blessed that I have integrated the one who loves to hug and express herself physically. It is a pleasure to have more choices of roles available and also to let them go. It is empowering be able to chose the roles we play instead of them controlling us.

3. Good, Evil, and Free Choice

"Only by contrast with evil could I have learned to feel the beauty of truth and love and goodness."

—Helen Keller

We need to take a comprehensive look at the whole concept of good and evil. To begin with, on a very practical physical level, the hypothalamus in our brain produces chemicals for every emotional experience, like anger, fear, joy, or compassion, and then releases these chemicals to send a signal to our cells, the smallest units of consciousness in our bodies. We get used to the chemicals, addicted to them, and we keep repeating the same patterns, craving more of what we have already produced. As we keep loading a cell with the same chemical attitude, it will produce a sister cell with more of the same enzymes.

A murderer has loaded his cells with more and more hate chemicals and continues this pattern ad infinitum. The only thing that can break the pattern is realizing his own desire for the chemicals released by vulnerability and love. The bottom line for the sexual deviant who murders a victim is the power over, and the utter surrender and vulnerability of, the victim. The vulnerability is experienced outside himself in the victim, but in fact he is intricately dependent and interrelated. Without that vulnerability in action he would not feel the intense pleasure he feels. His pleasure would be infinitely greater if in fact he owned his own vulnerability and surrendered to divine love himself. The chemicals that produce the rush through addiction to violence, pornography, and drugs pale in comparison to those of true bliss. The bliss brought on by surrender to pure love is profoundly ecstatic. We can rewire our brains to create different, healthier choices.

Ultimately the human race must learn to develop a relationship with our conscience. When we learn to live responsibly with an eye out for the wellbeing of our soul we experience the true bliss which comes from love, gratitude, and social connectedness. Not only does this have the power to transform our own brain chemistry, it also has the power to lift others, and ultimately it is the only way to transform humanity in terms of constructive evolution of consciousness.

Any hope of changing as an individual lies in being aware and conscious in the moment. Then, when we decide to let go of beliefs which keep us at the lower energy vibrations, we create new neuro-networks, new territory in the brain on a higher vibrational level. These connections then start replacing the old ineffective paradigms. We are, in effect, rewiring our brains to create new choices. What we do to our minds is also what we do to our bodies. As soon as we rewrite our script in a way that elevates our energy levels with actions fueled by higher vibrations, we rise above what has happened before. Step by step, we gain more momentum towards a higher consciousness. We lose our old identity, personality constructs, or ego, and create our own new reality. We can then function at a level of powerful intention and manifestation. For instance, my brain is functioning as a powerful receptor for bliss now, and I am not complaining. When my Good Spot is in action all my senses, including the sixth, are keen and alight. I'm full of stars and closer to God than ever. We want to aim to produce the good chemicals, so we can load our cells with them.

It all boils down to choice. "Evil" can actually provide us with opportunities to stay faithful to the health of our own souls, if we can stay true to ourselves, conscious even in frightening or threatening situations. If we refuse to shrivel from fear and instead stay open to the source of love, evil will have lost its power.

And what about "good"? Good is that which is life-affirming. Religions provide rules for life based on the values of treating others like we want to be treated. Ultimately though, each of us is totally responsible for creating the true wellspring of our soul, lived out truthfully with the spirit of compassion and love.

I believe Satan is a word for the temptation within us; we have a choice to succumb to it or not. The unconscious people living at lower vibrations—people who hate, whose spirits have not yet returned to the light—have chosen to succumb to temptation more often than not. I like what Sylvia Browne says in *The Nature of Good and Evil,* "Stop with the devil. Quit giving him so much energy. Now, are there evil entities that roam the earth? Yes, they walk among us in suits and dresses, and they drive cars. They're not devils, they are mean people."

To protect ourselves from these kinds of people we need to become aware of the spectrum of frequencies available to us. Dr. David Hawkins, in *Power vs. Force,* discusses this spectrum of the levels of human consciousness by naming a range of values and emotions. He calibrates these according to attractor energy fields and vibrations. For instance, energy vibrations of optimism, forgiveness, and reverence for spirit are higher than greed or anger. When we stay in the higher vibrations we can actually convert lower energies to higher vibrations. Also, generally speaking, we attract what we emanate: this is a universe where "birds of a feather flock together".

In Dr. Wayne Dyer's book, *The Power of Intention,* he gives a list of suggestions for raising our energy vibrations so that our presence energizes others and we attract the love and kindness we want in our life. Both these books are full of inspiration for aligning our lives with creative, constructive vibrations.

Some helpful advice about evil:

1. Don't be intimidated. Realize the power we have by stepping out of the dominance/submission game and creating our own paradigm based on truth. We will find much support from others on that level of peace.
2. Choose carefully which movies we go to and which TV shows we watch. Movies with Satan in them scare people. Power people scare people. Scare and control tactics work to intimidate people. If we buy into that paradigm, we become victims.
3. Remember this: Nobody has the right to take our light, our confidence and our life direction away from us. We don't need to love unlovely people. We don't need to praise them, feel intimidated by them, or allow them to take over. We also don't need to hate them. We can let them live out their own lives. Focus instead on how we want to live ours.

Bad Boys/Good Boys: Trusting Intuition

When I was 13, I had my first real experience of the good and evil we all have inside of us, and my first evidence that I could tune in to my strength and intuition.

It was a warm summer evening and I was riding my bike home after spending time at the public swimming pool with my friends. This was a relatively new arrangement that my parents had finally agreed to. My mother, who was more lenient about my independence than my father, had warned me, "I've seen a motorcycle gang hanging around in the neighborhood and I don't trust them."

Super-confident, I had responded, "Mom, don't you think I can take care of them?"

"No, I don't think you can if they want to do you harm."

"No, Mom, they just drive around. I've seen them, they just want to look tough, they don't even look at me." I was convinced. Finally my parents relented, so, after swimming, I rode my bike straight home, enjoying the warm breeze, feeling proud of my independence.

When I arrived at the house, I needed to carry my bike down to the basement, which I did right away. As I started to make my way back up, three gang members stood on the stairs, blocking my way. I had not heard or seen them anywhere. This realization was a shock, since it meant they had been watching me and intentionally set out to catch me in this particular spot. These boys knew they would be unobserved, since the lower part of the house contained one of our stores on the main floor, while above it were our self-contained living quarters and in the attic were rooms for apprentices. At this time of night, my father was watching TV in the living room, while my mother was most likely soaking in the tub in her private sanctuary. This was a large, well-insulated house and nobody could hear what was going on in the basement unless they actually came down into it.

As I registered this in my mind and felt shocked by their boldness in invading my house, I started to feel afraid. I had looked at them before and seen the decency beneath their exterior, but where was that now? If only I could get a glimpse of that, I would not feel so forlorn.

The smallest of the three guys, a wiry blond fellow, was giving a running commentary while gripping my left arm: "She's slippery, it must be the suntan lotion. I can't get a good hold on her." I kept rolling my arms back and forth, giving the guy on the right the same problem, thanks to the lotion. He was wondering if picking me up would be a better solution. This is when I started to address the leader, who was facing me. I looked at him, taking in his face, darkly handsome, full lips, eyes intensely zooming in on me. He was tall and strong and his hands were brushing the outline of my budding body. I felt confusion, embarrassment, and gratitude for the wire cups in my bikini top, about which he voiced his discontent to the other two captors.

While they were laughing and getting more aggressive, I began directing questions to the leader. "What is it you'd like from me? A date? If that's what you'd like, you are totally doing it wrong. And have you thought about my father? He wouldn't survive the blow this would cause him if he found out I'd been harmed."

Encouraged by a slackening of their intense lust, I kept on going: "Have you thought about me, how this would affect my future? I will never be able to go ride my bike home alone again at night. My parents will keep me locked in the house. I will never see you guys again on your motorcycles or around the swimming pool, since I'll never be allowed to go there again. Do you really want that? I want romance in my life, don't you? This is not a way to feel romantic. I thought you were quite handsome, let me continue to believe in that."

My arms were still being held, but I noticed the two sideline guys losing interest. So did the leader. He looked at me disappointedly and summoned his partners to leave me be. The three of them were still hesitating, looking back, unsure what to do, but slowly making their way upstairs. They were almost at the door, my nerves now getting raw. "Leave," I was screaming inside, "please leave." It seems they got the message and finally I was able to slam the door and turn the key twice, breathless, heart jumping out of my chest. I ran upstairs to safety. Then I hesitated—I was not able to face my parents yet. I ran to the attic, where one of the female apprentices I was close to lived. She was 16 and I knew she would understand. She kept reassuring me, "You did the right thing," and calmed my nerves until I was ready to slip into my own room, saying as little as possible to my parents.

After that, the guys stopped hanging around the area. I rode my bike home with a friend and immediately locked the door when coming into the house, so there were some lessons there for me about self-protection. Months later, my mother read an article in the local newspaper to me which said that this particular motorcycle gang had raped several girls. My mother, pondering her intuition, said, "See, I was right about them after all."

"Yes and no, Mom," I said. "They never did anything to me." I never told her more about it. Her intuition was right after all, but so was mine: our consciousness picked up what was there. Those boys had both possibilities within them.

We are ruled by what we believe. If we expect people are out to get us, we will be faced with opportunities to support that belief. On one end of the continuum is the bully, who sees himself entitled to be aggressive and in extreme cases to take the life of somebody else. Murder provides the illusion of having control over somebody's life. The delusion is that the person is playing God, all-powerful. But the finality of ending a life by killing a body is as much an illusion as our old belief that the earth is flat.

Misguided Beliefs

The earth is the center of the universe.
—Ptolemy, second-century Egyptian Astronomer

Everything that can be invented has been invented.
—Charles H. Duell, U.S. Commissioner of Patents, 1899

Throughout history there have been countless such beliefs, later proved to be completely wrong. Initially the forerunners to new and greater knowledge bear the ridicule and resistance of the people holding on to the established belief. Many of us now still behave as if the earth is the center of the universe. This is how we justify our habits of succumbing to temptation. From that perspective, messing with evil makes sense to us. There are many vibrational levels we can choose to engage in: Shame, Fear, Anger, Courage, Love, just to name a few. Dr. David Hawkins calls these levels of human consciousness the hidden determinants of human behavior. The higher the vibrational level, the closer to Joy and Peace we come.

While writing about good and evil, I came across an article by Shelley Page, titled *Terry, Clifford and Me.* In it, she demonstrates how all the possible energies—from lowest to highest—are in close proximity simultaneously at any given moment. She used three stories sharing headlines in the paper as her illustration. One concerned Terry Fox, a local hero who ran across Canada with a prosthesis on one leg to raise money for fighting the disease that had claimed his leg. His mantra: "You can be anything you want to be." Terry Fox is a good example of how some people make a big difference in others' lives, affecting many by their energy field. He rose above pain to admirable levels of courage and determination. When Terry died he had already raised more than the $1 million he'd imagined. He is still inspiring a great many of us to reach for our strength and perseverance.

Another headline focused on Pope John Paul II who was saved, after he had been shot, by what he considers the guiding hand of the Mother of God. Some believe that the Pope's convictions and guidance from a higher power have a compensating effect on the greed levels of consciousness.

And finally Page mentioned the headlines about Clifford Olson, a serial killer. His low level of consciousness had a destructive force not only on society at large, but on himself. I believe that each individual has mixed intentions within us. Even Clifford Olson on some level wanted love, but he felt entitled to brutality. This brought him to a dangerous level of destruction. There may be a faint stirring of hope towards a meaningful life for Olson if he would face his temptations and reach deeply enough inside himself to validate his own sensitivity, and transcend his level of falsehoods. His victims, innocent young girls and boys, are symbols of the tremendous tragedy created by these destructive energy sources. Stories of innocents, Navin's included, act as compelling reminders which should awaken our own consciousness towards action. Standing up for sensitivity, for preserving and protecting innocence, must be a number one priority for us as individuals and for society as a whole.

Astronomers believe that only about 5 percent of the universe exists in the form of ordinary, light-producing matter that we can see with our eyes. About 25 percent of the remainder is believed to be some as yet unidentified matter, and about 70 percent an even stranger non-material energy. In other words, we don't know what we are missing because we are missing it, it doesn't reach our eye. The choice is ours at any time, though. We can stay in the second century or move up to this millennium. We can gaze into the darkness of the universe and be exhilarated instead of frightened. We can cast the light of knowing upon that which is not illuminated to reach our physical eyes. If enough people learn to do that we can change our collective consciousness, and we will have fewer pools of misery to swim in and more an ocean of joy.

4. Claiming Our Sensitive Empathic Power

I believe that opening to what I call our Sensitivity—our sensitive empathic intuition—is the key to reaching a positive tipping point for the new paradigm.

As intuitives, we tend to give our power away. We would often rather walk out the door than face an uncomfortable situation. Intuitives are highly-tuned emotionally. Sometimes we try to hold our emotions in check so that we won't be ridiculed. Many sensitives are easily embarrassed, which takes up a lot of energy and prevents the excitement it takes to be in touch with the world.

As sensitive intuitives, we need to become comfortable with the fact that not everybody is supposed to like us. We need to focus on liking ourselves enough to be who we really are in the world. Paradoxically though, the more of ourselves we can bring out, the more people are attracted to us. The more we are able to show all our sides, the more our authentic honest and funny self can come through. The more we let ourselves express, the more we can initiate loving relationships. Shyness is a way of hiding our sensitivity from the world, and thus the world continuous to be deprived of the sensitivity it needs so much. Initiating love—giving love which is active and expressive—cures this shyness. We can begin by loving ourselves, in our entirety.

We need to understand that there are two basic motivators to human existence: to love and be loved. Knowing this, we can understand where our fear and anger come from—when something is blocking our loving or our being loved. Once blocked, usually it takes being heard and understood to be able to return to receiving and giving love.

We need to find a supportive environment where we feel others understand what it is like to be sensitive. This means we need to come out of hiding and give each other support.

"Warrior" is a term often used to describe finding the inner strength to act. Emotions are powerful motivators: they can help us to integrate all our personality parts with our spirit, to stand on our own two feet and come from the heart. The inner warrior can be released to say, "Enough is enough. I've had it with being a victim. I will no longer berate myself with negative self-talk. I will not allow myself to be co-dependent with anyone who is abusive. I won't let that degradation be part of my life."

What goes hand in hand with owning our power is having a well-developed success fund. Like a bank account, we need to make deposits to accumulate rewards—otherwise nothing happens. If we own our power, our intelligence, our sensitivity, we make consistent deposits to our conscious evolution. By engaging in self talk that is positive and life affirming, we grow our success fund. We say to ourselves, "Wow, I did get up. I've already brushed my teeth. I am ready to deal with my first priority today. I've already started writing. I've already written five sentences." We don't get a bloated ego from it, but it keeps us going and doing the work that needs doing. It's that kind of experience that leads to a flow of productive activity. We don't engage in a lot of negative self-talk, which is wasted energy, as simple as that.

People who feel successful are excited and alive. Who hasn't seen that energy in people and wanted to feel like that? The people with a well-established success fund, who make consistent deposits to earn rewards, see the world in a positive light. As sensitives, we tend to internalize our failures and externalize our successes. In other words, when something goes wrong we are quick to blame ourselves, but attribute successes to external situations. As successful sensitives we need to learn to internalize our successes, give ourselves credit for them.

Grow Your Success Fund

To begin growing our success fund, we can start by thinking of five successes in our lives. Then write them down and allow ourselves to feel the joy of our success fully. We need to be gentle and kind with ourselves when we celebrate our success. If we are shy, we need to recognize how we deprive others when we don't let ourselves be successful. We deprive ourselves and others of the power in our sensitivity.

When we are in fear mode, saying to ourselves, "I can't do it, I am not smart enough, strong enough, rich enough," etc., we can reframe our emotions. How can we grow if we put ourselves down all the time? We can get started by doing just one thing, and then celebrating it. Listen to our intuition, our power of intention, and our heart. When there is joy in our hearts we are on the right path. We need to learn to trust it!

Remember, everything is energy and it travels in frequencies and vibrations—and this includes emotions. So energy comes and goes. We can let it go if we decide to. Old blocked energy we have decided to hold on to may show up as something chronic in our bodies like tight muscles, stooped shoulders, ulcers, acne, or disease. Therefore, release is healthy. Release is not incessant venting or whining about how we have been wronged. Release is feeling the pain, the anger, or fear, giving it expression and moving through it, leaving it in the past.

Expressing and letting go of our anger, sadness, and fear is like anything else, it's all quick-moving energy unless we block it and hold on to it. When we hold on to our old hurts and grudges we practice the art of being right and the art of bitterness that lasts. It's a way of functioning that society has adopted in the past, but it is no longer serving us. We need to change that paradigm. To dwell on anger and fear is the root of self-destruction.

Everything we attend to expands. As our success fund grows, we search out more and bigger successes continuously. Our growth will accelerate exponentially when we get used to attending to our successes, learning to nurture them instead of our failures. After all, what we nurture grows, whether it is our failures, our problems, or our successes. Our choice lies in what we want to expand.

New Paradigm Principles for Living

Most of us habitually look outside ourselves to solve our problems: we consult experts to tell us what is wrong with us, and we tend to blame the world for our misfortunes. But in the new paradigm we look to our own worldview as both the cause of our condition and the cure. We become our own agent for change—and by doing so, we positively affect the world around us. When we see a need for change, we make that change happen by tuning into pure intelligence fuelled by the energy of a loving heart: we trust intuition because we know we are all connected.

Historically, women have been considered the torchbearers of intuition, empathy, and the belief in the oneness of all things; at the risk of sounding gender-biased, I have observed that men tend to want scientific proof and rational explanations for the intuition that offers solutions. Thankfully, this seems to be changing now that many are recognizing the positive results that inner knowing often gives. Part 3 of this book will give you concrete exercises to try that will help you to develop your intuition.

Tuning into our intuitive guidance, though, is not enough: we need to change our level of consciousness—raise our vibrational frequency, if you will. As more people embrace the concept that everything is energy and frequency, more of us are empowered to change it so we can be aligned with the desired results. How do we change our frequency? First and foremost by making a conscious change in our thought-patterns. In the simplest terms, the effect of thinking *hate* is very different from the effect of thinking *love*, and we can choose to think *love*.

Here is an example from my practice. Today, I saw a client who personified the effect of thinking *hate*. He kept speaking about his ex-wife in terms of great antipathy. His open hostility towards her had created a mutually distressing situation where both felt the need to protect themselves from the other.

He told me that he was going to wrap up his divorce first and then move on with his life; my client was clearly putting off the idea of doing any good in the world until *after* the divorce. It became clear as he spoke about his past experience that there will always be another obstacle in his life that will evoke his hatred and so yet another reason to postpone his much-needed change in consciousness. The client felt suspicious about the whole idea of positive energy. He told me that he had tried and tried to be positive, but nothing worked: his ex was still the same shrill madam, and he was still as angry and frustrated as ever.

This client needed to hear that the fundamentals of the new paradigm have nothing to do with putting on a smile, or "trying to be positive." They have to do with *living* the loving thoughts, with treating others the way you would like to be treated. If my client could spend even half as much time sending his wife healing energy as he now spends sending her destructive energy, she would be much more inclined to treat him with civility.

Anything we focus on will grow. Here is something you can try: change your thinking about one person you are having a difficult time with. Send that person positive, kind thoughts and empathy. No matter how hard you may find this, continue and persevere with it. Integrating new paradigm principles into our daily lives takes persistence: spending five minutes thinking kind thoughts is a good start, but it won't be enough; to align our wavelength, we need consistent effort. Fortunately, interactions and events will eventually prove to you what a positive difference you are making in your life with your efforts. Conversely, if you say, "I don't believe this, the person I'm thinking of will never change," you will be right. Whatever we believe and concentrate on will grow.

The most powerful energy in the universe is loving energy, oneness, heart-thinking. We block this energy by not accepting its power, or by condemnation, judgment, fear, trying to explain, shame, and aggression. But every loving thought heightens your potential and that of the world around you.

Pure love creates no resistance, it just is. When we fight, we feel powerful: we felt the resistance but we overcame it! Fighting creates the illusion that we are doing something—there is lots of noise and action, and we confuse that with results, but the feeling of triumph is short-lived. The true results we yearn for are not created by fighting but by love. God is love, human beings are rational, and our true challenge as humans is to have faith in love and embrace being one with the greatest power in the universe.

ACCESS: Acronym for Living the New Paradigm

The fundamental principles of living the new paradigm are a lens through which it is easy to access thoughts, words and actions in a loving energy spectrum. This kind of big-picture thinking is necessary to help us realize our most fundamental desires: to be loved, connected, and at peace.

Here is a simple way to remember the language of loving energy manifested in thoughts, words, and actions: ACCESS

Appreciation - Appreciative words, thoughts, and feelings, thoughtful actions, friendly sharing, empathetic listening, a gentle touch, and kind deeds.

Compassion - Having others' best interests at heart, concern for the well-being of yourself and others. Compassion and empathy open the channel to guidance for your own personal growth.

Choice - You are human, so it is inevitable that you will feel angry, self-righteous, blaming, and self-pitying on a regular basis. But you have a choice: you can bring yourself back to the new paradigm of oneness and serenity by letting go of those negative thoughts, words, and actions. Change "I can't" to "I won't" and then choose to think ACCESS instead.

Energy - Go with the flow of growth and life-expanding energy. Remember that everything is energy, so you can let go of those energy blockers which prevent you from accessing the peaceful universal mind.

Shift - Be self-disciplined. When you notice yourself repeating the same old self-defeating patterns of thinking, using unkind words, and acting in restrictive ways, be smart and signal yourself to stop: tell yourself, "Enough is enough." Be your own positive but firm mother-father, teaching you how to stay in the realm of good vibrations. Stop blaming your parents or others for failing you: it is up to you to be your own best teacher.

Spirit - When you shift to the abundance mindset of the new paradigm, you realize that you are unlimited. You and the cosmos are one, without end. How could there be an end to the universe? Where would it be? It's like saying the world is flat. You came from an unlimited consciousness. Practice being simply and peacefully receptive to the infinite power that created you.

Here are a few additional guidelines:

* Look for books that give you tools to access more life-affirming ways. For instance, I recommend Gary Chapman's *The Five Love Languages* as a succinct guide for the words and actions that are most helpful in relationships.

* Take the word "don't" out of your vocabulary; the inner self does not hear it, only the phrase that follows. For instance, when you tell your children, "Don't cross the street without looking," they hear "Cross the street without looking." Instead, say "Stand, look for traffic, and then cross the

street when it's safe." The same principle applies to the adult mind: it needs tools that tell it positively what to do. Hearing all the "don'ts" only encourages the mind to expand on the negative.

* Embrace the big picture of the new paradigm so you can stop "sweating the small stuff" as Richard Carlson says. The larger perspective enables us to move forward, clarifying our inner desires, and creating ways to realize them in the world.

* Criticize less, accept more, send out constructive and healing thoughts, let go of the desired results, and have faith. Then you are at peace with yourself and the world around you.

This is living in the new paradigm.

PART 3

A Guidebook for Belonging

When we become more open, our lives expand with the sense that we are part of an infinite network and joined in countless ways. For me, as I lived each moment as an exciting new discovery, I felt a new love growing, a new sensitivity about beauty which I had never felt before. As I became sensitive to the world as a whole, this created new relationships for me, not just with people but with the birds, the oceans, the stars. Life became richer and friendlier as my appreciation grew.

When I started living in a more soulful way, in conscious appreciation of the network that connects all things, I began receiving clear guidance and help. That guidance is available to all of us. For me, the guidance often came in dreams, but I was also learning from others' stories, as they shared with me their experiences on the path. I share some of these stories with you now, as more real-life examples of new-paradigm living, along with practical exercises for becoming more sensitive and open that you can try yourself. All of us can become clear and open channels for the great power that connects us all.

Stories As Healers and the Healing Power of Love

All through my growing up, my father never spoke about his Holocaust experiences, but I knew they were there like a dividing wall between us. Neither of us would touch the painful memories that would make him grumpy during the day and keep him from sleeping at night. But one day, when I was about sixteen, Dad started to talk. I had told him I had no respect for him and was not going to listen to him anymore. This triggered such sadness in him that he could no longer contain himself, and the wall tumbled down.

"You know," he said "that I was in Bergen Belsen."

This really got my attention: I couldn't believe he was finally bringing it up.

"What you don't know," he continued, "is how I felt there. I had suffered a severe case of typhoid—many of us in the camp were sick with it—and I was totally emaciated, from that and from starvation. But it didn't matter. I was forced to work long hard days in the fields. I was sixteen." My age! As he told me these details, I could feel my teenage reserve melting rapidly.

"We were forbidden to eat anything we might have found while working the fields," he continued. "We were told we would be shot if we didn't follow orders, but occasionally there would be a temptation, such as an old potato overlooked in the harvest or an edible root of some sort that nobody dared to pick up."

My father and his friend came across an old potato one day. "When I saw it, my hunger became so strong I almost fainted," he recalled. "But I pulled myself together and told myself to think, Alex, think. All I have to do is pick it up, get it into my mouth and chew away at it very slowly, savor it while it lasts."

"Did you pick it up?" I asked.

"I almost did," he replied, "But you know me, I'm always cautious. I looked around carefully. There was a German guard who was looking in the other direction. I watched him like a hawk to see if he was going to turn around."

"I guess he didn't turn around," I assumed.

"He did," said my Dad. "My friend had seen the potato too, remember. He had watched the guard, also, and he was faster than I. When he bent down, the guard shot him on the spot. First, the Germans invaded our house and our land, they shot my three German shepherds, my father was executed for his possessions, and I never saw my mother and brothers again. Then, I lost my friend over a dirty old potato."

At this point, my father started to shake uncontrollably. I held him close and we cried in each other's arms. The pain was so deep and powerful, we shook and struggled, both of us feeling a bottomless sorrow and unable to stop it. Until then, he had not touched the pain out of fear that we could not stand it—when he was finally able to speak about his experience, it was as if a dam had broken. But the tears and the release actually brought us closer. Eventually we both calmed down, and rested in a feeling of deep peace. Being heard and loved in the midst of pain and sorrow is a gift: love truly does heal all wounds.

Over and over I have seen in my practice, and in my own personal life, that having the courage to confront pain by speaking about it—telling the story in the presence of someone who can receive it with empathy and love—is one of our most powerful healers. I encourage all of you to find a compassionate witness and share your stories with each other.

In this photo taken two years after his liberation from the concentration camp, my father is in the front row, on the far right. Everyone in the photo is a Holocaust survivor. I think this picture shows that survivors weren't necessarily the strongest people physically, but were often the spiritually strongest.

Bliss

In Part 1, I promised you the story of my own personal epiphany. I share it with you now in the knowledge that each of us can experience the same intensely beautiful joy.

My Bliss Experience: The Good Spot

Have you ever read about an experience of bliss and ecstasy so intense that, afterwards, nothing was ever the same again? I had read many such accounts, and I had thought that such experiences were only available to mystics who spent decades meditating in remote Himalayan caves, or chanting mantras by the hour. But I was wrong.

Not long after the Dream Voice experience and the connection with Navin, I had one of the most intense and exciting experiences of my entire life.

Here is the journal entry I wrote about it:

"In a half sleep, I become aware of a spot just past the middle of my head on the right side, which feels soft, vibrant, illuminated and strangely expansive. Then my awareness expands to my body. It is so sensitively charged, in a state of extreme bliss. There are tiny explosions of light around me and through me. I breathe slowly and steadily and the iridescent sparklers keep falling into me, into my arms and fingertips, and radiating throughout my whole body. Only the slightest of focus on that blissful state brings it about. These tiny explosions of light like fireworks go on and on throughout my body. I am ecstatic. It's a mystery to me. My heart is free. I feel like I can do anything. I'm not bound to a physical body, in fact, my body is irrelevant, and I'm thankful for that. Spirits exist on another dimension; we can transcend this space and time. My mind is freed. I am without limitations. Bliss is all around. My eyes move involuntarily, as if in the deepest of dreams, but I am not sleeping. It is blissful and orgasmic even though it has not been brought on by a sexual experience. It's a mystery to me. I am charged full of energy.

There is no need to hold on, no need to do anything but to watch in awe. I know this is one of those life-altering moments from which I can never turn back. I can only go forward into a new world. It changes the course of my life forever. I can only tell you, it was one of those moments of profound significance that confirmed a greater knowledge of truth than I ever thought possible. I've been taken over by a swirl of events with incredible momentum.

This Good Spot in my brain, which feels so strangely expansive, resonates with such depth and sensitivity in my body that I am totally enveloped by unconditional love inside and out. My life has become more and more about love, internally I've been continuously letting go of control and opening myself. Passion is flowing. I feel galvanized, a burst of renewed intention. I want to touch humanity. I want to make a difference in the world. In this state, it all seems possible."

I found out that the ecstatic experience is profoundly orgasmic, a peak spiritual event combined with an extremely intense blissful and prolonged whole-body sensation. It is extraordinarily beautiful. You keep falling and falling into more rapturous, electrifying, orgasmic energy from head to toe. But these transcendental experiences go beyond sexuality: they are an opening to the Source of love. There are many people who have experienced this phenomenon and reported it; even if they were skeptics before, afterwards they could no longer argue with it.

Since my own experience of bliss, I truly know that there is nothing to be afraid of. Light conquers the dark if you can just let it in, and all it needs is a tiny opening. Being with the light energy of compassion, forgiveness, and love means you will overcome all that is false. Love is the world's most powerful force. You have to let go of the ego and the compulsive details of daily life to experience the burst of inner radiant energy that is bliss. The mundane aspects of life still exist;

they are necessary. It is important work to hold down a job, clean the house, fix dinner, pick the kids up from school, do the laundry—but these tasks are not the only essence of life. Work is the mechanical part of being, and it has to get done, but when you know the true essence that is driving you, you are in alignment with your true purpose. Ask yourself: Is it greed, fear, or love that fuels my motivation to do? If the answer is love, bliss is on its way.

I can imagine a world where everyone is connected to the ecstasy of this divine bliss, rather than seeking its pale counterfeit in alcohol, drugs, or other addictions. In fact, I believe that it is our universal human longing for that bliss that drives us to addictions of all kinds. But no drug in the world can compare with the ecstasy of true rapture. And it is good to remember that, although these experiences feel miraculous and extraordinary, they are actually our natural state of being. This is what life is supposed to be like: you have a sense of limitless possibility; you are in a realm of utter trust and know you are safe. It is clear that you are not your body, but that you have one to contain you. There is no fear. When it ends you actually feel refreshed, cleansed, cleared. You see the rest of your life differently. Your petty little worries have assumed their proper proportion in your life and you realize that what truly matters is a life with purpose—a life where you are open to the abundance and the goodness of the universe.

Inviting Bliss In

In 2002 I had seen a client twice who was rather guarded in her approach to life and to what I had to say. About 2 years later, shortly after I had my Bliss experience, I was surprised to hear from this client again. She told me she had made many positive changes since she last saw me, but she was living on her own and wanted to feel less lonely. She hoped I could help her with the relationships in her life.

Together we discovered what kept her from attracting what she really wanted. She had been dabbling in some S and M relationships with bondage and found those quite exquisite. She feared that a regular kind of relationship could not compare with the intense pleasure and heightened excitement she felt in those S and M scenarios. What she did not like about it was the humiliation factor and the game-playing, which prevented her from forming a good long-term relationship.

Since her returning to me occurred shortly after I had my profound ecstatic experience, I could honestly tell her that it was possible to have this intense heightened state of bliss without all the bad side effects. This got her attention. Since I do know about a spiritually centered relationship and how good the sexual experiences are on that level, I kept on telling my client about that. So we went on an exploration of the art of loving that engenders a much more powerful, prolonged, and intense pleasure than any other experience known to man or woman. This is what the G-Spot experience is in this life, the Good Spot in the brain, the soul and body united. The vulnerable spot which, when treated gently with tender care, responds with exquisite bliss that transcends space and time.

We spent time defining what it meant to align herself with the loving heart space which would attract this experience. The more pure, focused and intended this energy is, the more aligned we are with the force to attract this energy. When we focus on the lonely heart and the deprived soul, the more we are aligned with that negativity. Remember it is like the magnetic forces all around us: if we are not enough in alignment with the force we want to attract, we will actually repel it!

This was a big "Aha!" for my client and she felt inspired to try it. We had a couple of reinforcement sessions where she kept getting better and better at knowing what she wanted in her life.

A few weeks later she came back to tell me that she had taken up with an interesting, kind man from California whom she had known for awhile. She had held herself back from a relationship with him previously, since she thought she would sabotage it as she had done in the past with men she had actually cared for. Now she had confidence that she could actually have a real relationship, with ups and downs, but with the love and respect she had always yearned for. She felt she could trust herself now, since she had become much more patient and loving, and she felt ready to continue that path with this man. He came to visit her, and she him, and after six months she moved to California to be with him. I am confident she will have a great life with him if they both continue to bring themselves back to the path they found together.

Better Than Drugs

Around the time of my own intense bliss experiences, a mother called who was referred to me by another client. The mother told me over the phone that her 21-year-old daughter was listless, couldn't hold down a job, and was generally very depressed. When I opened my office door I was looking for a heavyset, sad girl on my couch. To my surprise, there was a slender, rather alert-looking person waiting for me.

As I started interviewing her about her life, we soon got to the heart of the matter. This young girl had not fit into the system at high school. She finally found a small group of peers she felt comfortable with. The problem was that this group had created a center of acceptance for each other under the influence of cocaine. There they could escape from the cliques and the everyday pressures into an exciting other reality.

When I validated this young woman's sensitivity, her artistic ability, and her striving to get away from the current paradigm, she shook her head in disbelief. "Why hasn't anybody ever told me this before? I always felt so out of place. With my friends I felt safe, but I also felt terribly guilty, letting myself and my family down."

We spent the next sessions exploring what it meant for this client to align herself with her own sensitivity and the excitement it generates. She told me of her deep aspiration: to get involved in set design. Her teachers had greatly encouraged her artistic abilities, but she had not allowed herself to feel the enthusiasm that comes along with pure inspiration.

In the safe place we created for this expression of sensitivity and inspiration to occur, she found her inner peace and confidence in her abilities. The joy she felt was ongoing and so much more rewarding than the short-lived artificially-induced high from drugs. The client told me she wouldn't dream of going near cocaine again, because it just wasn't necessary any longer. Her inner peace and artistic inspiration are stretching her mind and keeping her stimulated. With so much passion in life, she has no room for depression.

Transcendent experiences of bliss are so much better for us than drugs—and we can actually produce them ourselves. Also, there is nothing illegal about them!

Bliss in Our Culture

Dr. Spencer Nadler, in *The Language of Cells*, helped to confirm my own personal bliss experience by suggesting that the creation of alternate neural circuits in the brain can effectively bring about orgasm. In his own words, "Though ejaculation is primarily a genital event, orgasm is primarily a cerebral one."

This experience of bliss, rapture, or ecstasy is very different from the purely physical arousal based on sexual stimulation or images and fantasies. Our culture engages mostly in a very physical form of sexual arousal. This type of stimulation is in turn supplying the negative chemicals which keep us addicted to more. We are bombarded with visual imagery of macho men and anorexic women engaging largely in seductive and debasing sexual activity. We end up craving this type of sexual arousal, producing more of the same enzymes. Addiction to porn, violence, and fear is consistently escalating the need for more of the same. This is the nature of addiction: each time, we need a bit more to get a buzz.

We have over-sexualized and under-sensitized the world. Sensitivity is highly undervalued, but where are we without it? Steeling ourselves and pretending not to feel is what causes so much of our misery. All forms of aggression are associated with the numbing of pain but also the numbing of pleasure—real pleasure and bliss.

In his book called *Dreams That Have Changed the World*, Dr. Robert Van de Castle quotes Ken Kelzer, who claims that the benefits of lucid dreaming include providing people with a natural (no drugs or chemicals) experience of ecstasy. "The ecstasy that I refer to seems to run the whole gamut of human possibilities - from intense sensual delights, indescribable orgasms and pleasures, to peak-spiritual experiences and everything that people can possibly imagine... I have come to appreciate more clearly that human beings need ecstasy in one form or another."

Experience Bliss Yourself

You attract bliss experiences when you bring more and more unconditional love into your life on a daily basis. Keep reminding yourself of ACCESS, especially when the going gets tough. Also try and fix the areas in your life that keep you away from living authentically, apologise when you have wronged somebody, like your children or your spouse or other significant friend. It is then the deepest letting go of pride happens and unconditional love can take its place.

All falseness falls away, no effort is required when we rise beyond our conditional constructs of daily posturing just before we go to sleep. In this still silent place, with our eyes focused on the heart, we can feel a peace, a stillness and fullness.

Let appreciation and gratitude fill your soul. See your child really happy or your spouse or friend in their true loving essence. Picture yourself beside them with the release from false pride and daily "shoulds". Before you go to sleep, feel the gratitude and let a buzz of appreciation fill your heart. Allow yourself to sink into that restful space and drift into sleep.

For many of us, after we wake in the morning and before we get out of bed is the easiest time to access the ecstatic energy of blissful unconditional love. As you put out your intention towards attracting more bliss into your life you will find more stories and poems that tell you how other people have had their transcendent experiences. This will help bring about your own profound experiences in this energy field of light.

Deep Dreaming

Reading about Friedrich von Kekule, a Belgian professor of Chemistry, made me aware of just how much dreams are currently misunderstood and undervalued. For a long while, Kekule had been fruitlessly trying to figure out the structure of the benzene molecule. One night, he fell asleep in his armchair and dreamed of a snake that had seized its own tail. He awoke "as if by a flash of lightening:" his dream had given him the answer—the molecule was in the shape of a ring. His discovery subsequently revolutionized organic chemistry. Not surprisingly, he addressed a scientific convention in 1890 by urging the audience "Let us learn to dream, gentlemen, and then we may perhaps find the truth."

After my own awakening with the Dream Voice, I started recording my dreams every morning to see if they would reveal anything else. Usually this would have been a chore for me, but it wasn't now: my dreams were so exciting and vivid that I was compelled to write them down. I loved the process and began looking forward to going to sleep and dreaming. It was clear to me that I was receiving information on another level, without the judgment and barrier of the logical mind that dominated my waking hours.

I put a brand new notebook by my bed, ready to record whatever I remembered from the night. The writing itself was like taking dictation from a source outside myself: I felt like a vessel or vehicle. I was not thinking about the words—they were pouring out of me, through the end of my pen and onto the page. When I recorded these dreams, I had a profound sense that they came from a source with unlimited knowledge. I did not question or speculate; I just trusted the process.

I believe that these dreams came to me because I had begun honoring my sensitivity, allowing it to be more present with my family and my surroundings. I had opened myself to more love and appreciation from my environment in general, and felt more compassion, strength and serenity as a result. Beginning to experience this larger loving energy made me feel as if I had tuned into a radio channel with very powerful positive energy signals. There was a magical glow to my life which made a material-bound world pale in comparison.

My voice dream made one thing very clear to me: once we get a message like this, it is imperative that we listen. It is our responsibility to be open and to learn who we really are. The door to other worlds had opened for me and I felt safe and happy. The message demonstrated great care for the human race, and that was good! It became a joyful task to be the scribe for the Great Mystery's messages to us.

Dreaming My Father's Death

Sometimes people fear dreams, in case they tell them something they are afraid of. I've heard many people say, "What use are dreams that tell me something horrible is going to happen? What good does it do, if there's nothing you can do to prevent it?" The fact is, even if you are not able to prevent an occurrence, the prophetic dream, where we witness the future during sleep, can help us prepare for and handle difficult situations.

Let me tell you my own experience with this and you can judge for yourself.

On March 11, 2005, I woke up in the morning, recalling a vivid dream. *I came to our house and the red door was slightly ajar and it was dark and empty inside. There was a note stuck to the door and an alarm system above the note. I was hoping we were protected from the break-in that way. I was afraid of the darkness inside and afraid to find out what happened.*

Then I had another dream right after that: *A girl is taking her dad to the museum. He goes upstairs, seems well, but suddenly passes out. He is white and collapses. She catches him, holds him in her arms, bends down on her knees and a sob escapes her chest. She revered her dad, she touches his left leg as if to hold on to him. Not sure if he is slipping.*

Then there is another sequence with an image of a spiral spinning and spinning. As I look closer, it is made of little balls, somehow related to pool balls, a design in a triangle, though a different material from pool balls, more ancient. This feels like a release compared to the first dream.

One year after my dream, my mom and my dad went for a walk on his birthday, near their home in Straubing, Germany. Suddenly, he complained of not being able to lift his left leg. He could barely walk, though somehow they made it home; my mother pushed and half-carried him up the stairs, and his leg seemed not to be working at all. To this day she still does not understand how she managed to get him upstairs, since she is a petite woman. She got him into the living room, where he collapsed. She says he folded up like a baby, with no control over his body at all. She called the ambulance and they took him to the hospital.

My father went through many tests and nobody could determine if he would recover. He went in and out of consciousness and neurologists tried to determine if he was still coherent. He could not tell what a pen was, but when asked if he had children, he managed to say very clearly: "One daughter, her name is Elke. She lives in Canada and she is a psychologist."

My mother kept hoping he would pull through and we kept debating if I should come to Germany right away. We had just moved into our new home and I was in the middle of renovations. Our old house was empty, just as it had appeared in the first dream. I was feeling very anxious, not only because of my father's health, but because the move and renovation were stressful. In consultation with my family I decided to leave for Germany anyhow, just in case my father would not recover.

But the night before I was due to leave, my mother called and was optimistic. "He pulled out of it today," she said. "He squeezed my hand and said clearly 'I'll see you tomorrow.'" I felt happy and wondered if I could stay home, but somehow, guided by my dream, I felt compelled to go anyhow.

When I arrived at my mother's house, she rushed me straight to the hospital. Her optimism had been unfounded; Vati was dying. I held and stroked him and told him how proud I was of him. I told him he did well, I was here now and it was okay for him to do whatever he needed to do. It seemed he could not understand any words at all, but he clearly had a hard time leaving, he was holding on to our hands. Finally it was time to let go.

His expression when he passed over was lovely, with a slight smile; he looked young and very calm. I could actually feel his release, so similar to the release I felt in the dream with the spiral.

This is an example of how a predictive dream enabled me to be there for my dad at just the right time. Considering my own anxiety and how optimistic my mother was, I would not have left my home if I had not felt the signposts from the dream guiding me along the path. Clearly, I needed to be there for my mom and my dad when he had to leave us.

Decoding Dreams

Dreams offer us a way to solve problems, gain insight into ourselves, and receive messages. Our dreams speak through symbolism, but then humans are symbol-makers, using symbols to communicate, from early cave drawings, religious symbols, and Chinese lettering to traffic signs and corporate advertising. The symbol language of dreams is especially mysterious and fascinating.

Here is an example of working with a dream to glean its significance. My daughter Sasha shared this dream with me:

Our whole family was in an airplane going to Australia. Our house had burned down. Sashika and Coco, our pets, were with us, though they were not a cat and a bird anymore but cocoons—and they transformed into many beautiful moths. The whole process took eight weeks. I thought at first it would take eight months and I was surprised that it was so quick."

We usually rely on a helpful book—*The Complete Dream Dictionary*, by Pamela Ball—to gain perspective on a dream's significance, so we began researching the images together. According to Ball, buildings represent the structure we try to give our everyday lives—our attitudes and beliefs that are experience-based. These burned down in the dream: there is change and renewal taking place. Coco, as bird, represents the soul, or vehicles for the soul. Sashika, as cat, represents the sensuous, powerful, self-reliant aspect of a woman. Transformation of animals in a dream means the potential for change in any situation. Airplanes signify a swift and easy journey. The cocoons hatching into moths connoted the freed soul and immortality. Moths are symbols of the hidden side of the Self, the nighttime, dreaming self. In the dream, Sasha had thought it would take eight months, but it only took eight weeks.

I believe that this dream pointed to Sasha's personal transformation, since she was then on the cusp of becoming a woman. It seemed positive to me that the transformation took much less time in the dream than Sasha had thought it would. Though it may seem scary to have our house burn down in the dream, the message here was about growth rather than preparing for a cataclysmic event.

Dreams continue to inspire and guide my life; in fact, it was a series of very specific and detailed spiritual guidance dreams that led me to the publisher of this book.

Dreams and Visions

In his book *Creative Dream Analysis,* Dr. Yamamoto divides dreams into three categories:

1. Physical/Emotional Clearance Dreams
2. Spiritual Guidance Dreams
3. Psychic Dreams

In physical/emotional clearance dreams, the inner intelligence of our subconscious gives us messages and symbolically recreates the pressing issues of our waking lives. For example, if you have suppressed your anger at somebody, you may have anger expressed in your dream. This can help you look for solutions on how to deal with the problem effectively.

If we recognize the problems described in a dream and we take some problem-solving actions, our dreams become increasingly empowered and lucid. As positive change occurs in our lives, dreams can evolve into spiritual guidance dreams.

Spiritual guidance dreams help us to evolve. They reveal what we have overlooked and what we need to do to correct the issue. This type of dream is easy to recognize because it is out of the ordinary. After my initial dream of Navin, more and more of my dreams became this type.

Dr. Yamamoto also talks about transcendental dreams, which stagger our imagination and totally put us into another world, another level of existence. They are the extraordinary dreams that defy casual description. Like near-death experiences, many people who have transcendental dreams report subsequently changing their lives in accordance with higher spiritual purposes. These dreams are exhilarating, joyful and transforming. My own experiences of bliss and ecstasy could be considered examples of these.

Here are some other helpful distinctions about dreams, loosely taken from Sylvia Browne's *Book of Dreams*. These definitions were very handy as I learned to differentiate between my own prophetic, guidance and regular release dreams.

Wish Dreams: These are about our underlying feelings of desire or wish-fulfillment fantasy.

Release Dreams: These generally give us an infinitely expansive view of ourselves, of what's going on in our lives and of how we *really feel* about things. These can provide useful information, since they point out feelings that our conscious minds are often too busy, confused, or afraid to let us confront. They are usually the most disturbing and chaotic dreams we experience, but are helpful in disposing of emotional "garbage".

Prophetic Dreams: Here we witness the future during sleep. Every prophetic dream has two qualities in common: they are in color (although not every color dream is prophetic!), and the action in the dream takes place in sequence, with one event leading to another, which leads to another, in some kind of logical order. Unlike other kinds of dreams that can be hilariously random and incoherent, the prophetic ones unfold in the form of step-by step stories and, because of that, can usually be tracked more easily by the conscious mind later, when the dreamer is awake.

Visionary Telepathic/Astral Travel Dreams: Like Kekule's vision of the snake biting its own tail, these dreams offer information and problem-solving during sleep. Did you know that the theory of relativity came to Albert Einstein in a dream? Dreams have inspired everything from Thomas Edison's invention of the light bulb to Elias Howe's invention of the sewing machine. How many people know that George Friedrich Handel heard the last movements of an oratorio in a dream, and Rene Descartes had dreams in which he received new perspectives that had a profound effect on philosophy and mathematics? And countless "ordinary people" have dreamed true dreams of loved ones passing over or other events. Browne says that these dreams are proof of telepathy, of information coming from outside the self, and of astral travel when, released from the confines of the body, the spirit is free to journey anywhere on the network in the blink of an eye.

However you choose to think about dreams, the important thing is to hone your dreaming gift and honor the information dreams bring. Becoming more discerning about the music you listen to, the books you read, the insightful movies you watch, and the people who enhance your life, will open you to more inspired dreams.

Dream Deeply Yourself

Write Down Your Dreams

Keep a notepad and pencil beside the bed and get in the habit of writing down anything you remember as soon as you wake up. Research has shown that most dreams will fade from consciousness after as little as eight minutes, so get out the net and keep those dream-fish from wriggling away! Many of us find it helpful to write our dreams in the present tense and to give them titles based on the dominant action or image. Writing the date on which you dreamed them is helpful, too.

Think About Your Dreams

The conscious mind is not the enemy of deep dreaming. in fact, our conscious minds can help the dreaming process along in two ways: first, by asking for guidance before going to sleep. Then, when you receive a spiritual guidance dream, after you write it down, simply pay attention to it. Keep the dream in mind during the day, moodle around with it. Do some free-association: what does it remind you of? Then use logic and fact-finding to amplify its meanings; the internet can be a tremendous help with this. If you dream of an animal, for example, google it and learn about its habits. Linear analytical thinking combined with a meditative state will help us to receive the messages that are sent to us.

Maintain High Ideals

Hold yourself to high spiritual ideals in life and your dreams will reflect that. They then can bring you the greater wisdom of the collective subconscious and not just reflect your personality self.

Remote Viewing

This is a conscious-focusing technique, where you set an intention to "visit" someone in a deep state of relaxation in order to access information. This fascinating phenomenon can be misused, though, so proceed with caution here: psychic snooping on others is not okay. In fact, according to Sylvia Brown's book on dreaming, for 25 years, the government had been studying ways to get psychics to spy out information in the dream state, but finally concluded that they wouldn't sanction it.

Remote viewing is interesting because it brings the subconscious and the conscious mind together in teamwork. The conscious mind has to be still while the subconscious is receiving a signal from an object or location you are focusing on. Then the conscious mind is engaged in expressing the signal. When you check out your findings with the person you were visiting, you can quickly determine the accuracy of your subconscious powers.

My Mother's New Habits

When I first read about remote viewing, I was curious to see if I could do it. So I did the most benign thing I could think of: From my home in Canada, I went to my mother's house in Germany. I saw my Mom walking around her part of the house, and then walk into my old bedroom. There were some kind of bubbles coming out of her mouth and I realized she was talking to herself. I also saw a book open on the arm of the couch in another room.

Those were two distinct things I could check out, since my mother does *not* read books, only magazines and newspapers. She is also not in the habit of talking to herself. So I called and asked. She said she had in fact gone into my room to find a pen in my old desk because she wanted to write me a birthday card. She was talking to herself then, saying something about where is the pen that she was having trouble finding. She also confirmed that she has indeed taken up reading books now, after not doing so for at least 10 years, but only reads them a couple of pages a time, then marks them or leaves them open to be continued. When she does this, she leaves the book on the arm of the couch.

If you try remote viewing yourself by visiting a friend or relative, you can check specific details with them. You may surprise yourself. Most importantly, at all times be respectful and lovingly aligned with the person you visit.

The Power of Manifestation

> *"If you can imagine it, you can achieve it. If you can dream it, you can become it."*
>
> —William A. Ward

Making Visions Real: The Dream House

A lot has been written recently about the power of intention and the positive effects of visualization. I have seen many times how the act of setting a deeply-desired spirit-goal and backing it up by creatively imagining the outcome can bring that very outcome to pass.

Here is a great example, in a letter from my friend Jon, that shows how he did this in a startling way:

"My wife Roisin and I sat down to our anniversary dinner back in 1998 and, as we often did, asked ourselves the question, 'Where do we want to be in the future?' We had a habit of making goals to help us achieve those things we needed to. However, on this occasion, I said I would love to live in a waterfront home. I picked up a piece of paper and said, 'like this' and proceeded to sketch out what I had in mind. I drew a house with a pitched roof, a smaller attachment on the left, large rectangle windows top and bottom, a pool with hot tub on the corner, a sloping garden with steps leading down to a dock with a sailboat attached. The way I drew the picture indicated that the house was on an outcrop of land—a promontory of sorts. Well, that was in 1998.

"Fast-forward to 2005, when we made the decision to emigrate to Canada. We had been looking at real estate for many months but nothing appealed to us. Then one day our realtor, Paul, saw a property and emailed some photos. This seemed like the right one. We flew over from the UK, saw the property, loved it, bought it, and returned home—all within 36 hours.

"We then set about packing up our belongings for the big move. It was while packing up my filing cabinet that a folder slipped from my hand and the drawing from 7 years ago fell out onto the floor—as if it wanted to be found. I remembered it immediately and, having not seen it since I drew it, I picked it up and looked at it. I immediately felt a chill run down my spine and called to Roisin. We both looked at the drawing, then at the photos of the house we had just bought. The new house was waterfront on a promontory. It had a pitched roof, a smaller attachment on the left, large rectangle windows top and bottom, a pool with hot tub on the corner, a sloping garden with steps leading down to a grass bank directly opposite a marina. It was completely uncanny. At least 12 points of similarity existed between my drawing and the house we just bought.

"I've showed that drawing to many people. If I did not believe in destiny before, I do now. This is literally my dream house come true."

Visualizing in order to manifest is not daydreaming. It's becoming conscious of the existence of the pieces needed in order to attract the desired result. It is knowing what's necessary, tapping in, being open, and allowing the possibilities to enter the realm of consciousness. When we finally recognize these things consciously, they not only influence us, they also empower us to excavate and reveal even more. When we enter the process of manifestation, we are invited to ask for what we need in order to bring about what we desire because, if we are coming from our deepest loving desires, we are totally in sync with what the Universe desires for us. But there is another important takeaway about the process: you can visualize in partnership, in connection with others, and in doing so, the power to manifest is increased dramatically. Far from being the way to live a disconnected and selfish life, manifestation can be used to bring about positive change for the good of all.

Manifest for Yourself

Connect with Your Deep Soul-Desire

One of the reasons that we sometimes don't get what we think we want is that our desires are not in alignment with our deeper selves. If you tell yourself, for example, "I want to lose ten pounds," that's not a goal that your spirit is likely to embrace. First of all, it is not self-loving: there is an unconscious assumption that you're not alright at your present weight. A better way to frame this would be, "I want to be radiantly vital and healthy."

Our minds often think they have all the answers about what we want, when our hearts and spirits feel and know differently. And while you too can learn how to visualize living in a sprawling multi-million-dollar home or driving a shiny new Porsche, and these things may well manifest for you, they are not the keys to achieving true well-being, either for you or for the planet. They do not answer the deepest needs of our souls. What we most deeply need, both as individuals and as a race, is a connection to spirit, to compassionate conscience, and to healing. It becomes important to quiet our minds so that these quieter voices can be heard. Jon and his wife did not seek an ostentatious home with which to impress others; they just wanted the home that felt right for them. And so it found them.

Work on Knowing You Deserve

Many of us hold ourselves back when it comes to wanting things because we don't really believe that we deserve them. Patterns of inhibition and deprivation are set up in childhood, but it is our task as loving adults to re-parent our inner children and encourage them to dream big dreams from the heart and spirit.

Unfortunately, in our current society there is much confusion around abundance; many people feel that poverty is spiritual or at least virtuous. In fact, there is nothing spiritual about either poverty or wealth. Appreciation of the abundance dimension occurs when we create harmony between spirituality and materialism. True spirituality is waking up every day and finding life a blessing. Bitter people, whether rich or poor, are blocking this energy by continuing to feel unhappy. Being rich in the deepest sense means living in harmony with the blessings of the world.

Imagine in Detail

In order to manifest those things that are for your highest good, it is helpful to be as detailed as possible. You could draw it, as Jon did, or write a detailed description. Some people enjoy making collages of their dream goals: photos, magazine pictures, images from art magazines—all these can help you to express what it is you long for most deeply.

A Formula for Success

My own personal success formula goes something like this:

1) I have a goal with the clarity of vision in my mind. I believe I am capable of doing this, that it actually wants

to be accomplished through me, and I trust that I will learn about the details along the way.

2) There is passion in my vision. I'm motivated by that vision and it propels me forward.
3) I start working at it, researching, networking. I announce it and…
4) Now I'm committed. Now I can't let myself down and…
5) I throw myself behind it with focus and work like a fiend.
6) All along I trust my intuition, observing the flow of information, the synergy and how it all fits together.
7) I make myself vulnerable by taking risks of money, time, and, effort.
8) I am determined, persistent and don't give up until the project is completed.

All my significant achievements in life were accomplished using my personal success formula. You may want to try it yourself.

When we open ourselves to the divine intention for our lives, how can we go wrong? If the Great Mystery brought us here in order to accomplish certain things, we will be supported by that Mystery to do them.

SENSITIVE INTUITION AND EMPATHY

We must embrace sensitivity's many gifts and challenges in order to live the life that is waiting for us.

I believe that one vital key to creating a more positive and healed world for future generations lies in nurturing our sensitive empathy. The wonderful fringe benefits include bliss, heightened awareness and intuition, serenity, and vital excitement: true riches, rather than the empty material riches we have been taught to crave. When you decide to explore your own intuitive gifts, you become part of the solution—the positive tipping point—towards a healed future.

Have you ever wondered if you were intuitive? Have you been able to pick up on others' feelings or sensed the atmosphere of a room when you walked into it? Do words ever just effortlessly come to you, giving you guidance? Can you sometimes envision the solution to a problem clearly and instantly in your mind? You may already be developing your sensitive empathy. The good news is that opening to your own possibilities will have positive effects, both immediate and far-reaching, on your own life. It has certainly transformed mine in ways I could never have imagined.

Intuition in History

In earlier times extrasensory abilities were honored. For instance, the ancient Greeks sought out the Oracles of Delphi, which were revered by both the nobility and the general public. The Oracles were visionaries who interpreted the signs.

Nostradamus, a physician and famous visionary, advised the kings and politicians of his time and was very often accurate. The Catholic Church, however, clamped down on him and on other visionaries, burning many as heretics for having "ungodly powers." The Church was extremely powerful at that time and believed that people needed to be told what to do and how to behave. They also wanted to be the ones in charge. This put a lot of fear into people, as they were told not to believe in themselves or their own psychic energy.

Then, near the end of the 19th century, mesmerism (hypnosis) became very popular as did séances (calling in the spirits of the dead). Unfortunately, many abused this for money, using all sorts of gimmicks to grab people's attention. They felt people needed this drama to be entertained. Many frauds appeared to take advantage of the believers in the audience and of course eventually even the believers turned off to protect themselves. We are still vulnerable to frauds if we can't learn to stand up to them and validate our own sixth sense.

Becoming More Intuitive

Intuition starts as an inner knowing which defies the linear, measured and factual: it is a feeling, a hunch, without needing all the facts or details in a situation. There is often a sense of excitement, clarity, and conviction that the road to success will emerge—and all you need to do is to follow the road. Then, following that hunch, the physical world cooperates. The more you pay attention to those gut feelings and are comfortable with them, the clearer the inner voice, guidance, and inspiration become.

Extrasensory perception is an intensified version of intuition. Mediums, or channels, are simply people who receive information from spirit energy forms. The first step to becoming more intuitive is to become aware that there is a non-linear channel, which happened for me through my voice dream. When Navin's presence came through and a voice told me, "*This was an interracial, intercultural hate crime,*" I felt passionate about that dream and I took a risk by telling others about it. But I never sought to be a medium. In fact, sometimes early on I wanted to shut down when I had visions or premonitions. However, I felt that the value of staying open to where it might lead was greater than my fears.

The second step to honing intuition is to invite it in, allowing non-linear ways of knowing to become deeper, more guided, more directed. I have learned that when I invite guidance, I often receive answers. All I need to do is to listen quietly, be receptive to the inner voice, and have pen and paper ready. As I invite more information in, I become more of a channel, taking notes for Spirit. I notice that my handwriting is different when I receive this kind of information: it becomes slanted. It is a completely unique experience for me, a decided energy coming through, and my pen just moving along. I could not have done the writing just from my linear and logical brain: it is truly a combination of both the creative and the linear brain working together. When we validate and cherish our sensitivity, we invite in spiritual guidance.

How I Receive Intuition

I may be in the car listening to music when ideas, snippets of information, and pictures flood in. Often in the shower, when letting the water run and letting go of all my worries, thoughts, and pressures, ideas will come in word or picture form.

I don't know and don't really need to know where the information comes from. I do care, though, about tuning into light, divine essence, or whatever you call the life-affirming spirit. Doing so is a powerful protector that many, many people have experienced. What works for me is to think of everything—people, emotions, belief systems—as energy. I release any energy that blocks the light. If I work on a higher vibration than feeding my ego, the answers flow very freely. The trick is not to have to know the answers, but to be open to them. Then you often find the most amazing possibilities.

When receiving intuition, I look inward. If I intentionally meditate on receiving, I've been told my face is serene yet intense, my eyes may be half closed. It's as if I see nothing but a blank screen. My surrounding is a backdrop I'm aware of, but it's just there. Nothing matters at that moment. There is peace in that moment, a sense of calm, surrounded by space, infinite knowledge. Then I have an inner knowing that something is coming through, popping in. It's clear as a bell when a piece of information arrives. It may be in words, which I have to quickly catch on paper, yellow sticky notes or my notebook beside my bed. I sometimes have trouble keeping up with the writing!

Being intuitive can be a regular way of receiving information. We have our five senses to help us in the physical world. Intuition and receiving information through a sixth sense is just the way of accessing the vast reality and energy beyond the physical. Everyone has an intuitive ability, whether we are aware of it or not. Some just hone it and open to more and more of the knowledge available to us.

Visioning and intuition are closely related. A vision has a particular clarity that stands out in memory with the same distinct detail whenever we conjure it up. It is more of a still picture that seems etched into memory. There are so many things we forget on a daily basis but the clear image of a vision is unforgettable. A vision with its vivid characteristics can occur in a dream, during the day or you can hold a very clear goal like a vision in your mind.

For example, I have a dream about a hologram. It stands out as a vision in its three-dimensional quality as a particularly vibrant message. Subsequently when occurrences remind me of that image, I notice those. I don't judge them or analyze them, I just let them be. The occurrences and synchronicities usually clarify the vision and I learn more information. Accessing that information comes very easily. I will be just opening a book to that page or come across someone who gives me the information I am looking for. It's almost effortless, an accelerated learning. Time seems irrelevant and the process is very fast.

As I grow older, I have become more and more comfortable not knowing certain things for sure. I just trust that the truth will emerge. Following that knowledge has become a way of being and has its own powerful current.

I believe that moving away from our negative ways of being to an adaptive evolution into a higher consciousness of healing requires this one thing: more and more of us must embrace our sensitivity and open our own consciousness. When enough of us have done this, a critical mass will form, a tipping point so to speak, where the human race can evolve, transcending all of the misguided and limiting belief systems that are by their nature so resistant to change. It is good to remember that even paradigms as deeply entrenched as the belief that the earth is flat can and do change, eventually.

For the sake of brevity, I refer to sensitive empathic intuition simply as "Sensitivity." Here is some vital information about it.

What Sensitivity Offers Us

*** Sensitivity reduces stress.**

One of the most profound effects of validating and cherishing our sensitivity is that our lives become so much less stressful. Tapping into deep, nourishing spiritual guidance makes life lighter and simpler—we don't second-guess ourselves so much or agonize over decision-making. Instead, we feel gently and surely guided by a loving force that has our good in mind.

*** Sensitivity gives intense bliss.**

One of the fringe benefits of sensitivity is that you can have profoundly ecstatic, erotic and blissful experiences—like massaging the G-spot of the soul. This intense spirit-bliss is more pleasurable than you can imagine.

*** Sensitivity means you will never be bored again.**

Life becomes the most fascinating exploration, an adventure of epic proportions. You become the heroine or hero of your own life, discovering deep and meaningful insights about your life and Life in general.

*** Sensitivity energizes and enlivens us.**

Since I first opened my own inner channels, I have experienced an abundance of vital energy. I sometimes think we could use Sensitivity to power the world! You will find this to be true, as well: when we tap into the great Source, we never feel depleted again.

*** Sensitivity is a valuable gift to offer others.**

Most of us want to help those we love. Some of us have a deep desire to change the world for the better. When we hone our gift of sensitivity, we will have something of great value to offer.

What Sensitivity offers the world

*** Sensitives are adept at healing individuals.**

Because they understand and connect deeply with others, Sensitives have the capacity to cut to the heart of the matter. Here's an example from my own client practice: In one of my sessions with a couple, I noticed my rising irritation with the husband. I had observed him making many veiled comments designed to hurt his wife. He was clever, though; she believed he meant well and she generally aimed to please and appease him. At one point I turned to the man, looked him straight in the eye and told him, "Frankly, you are one of the most cleverly abusive people I've ever worked with." He paused for a moment in shock. Then he too looked straight at me and responded: "Thank you. I've waited my whole life for somebody to say this to me. I've always suspected it, but really nobody ever told me." After this moment of truth-telling, he was freed to show his sensitivity. His wife, who felt quite stunned by this revelation, took in his heartfelt apology. In the ensuing process, both were healed. She learned to become assertive instead of complaining and he became a much better man, openly expressing his affection to a wife he actually loved quite deeply.

*** Sensitives receive Visions that can heal and inspire.**

Sometimes Visions are meant to inspire the world, but they can also come to teach or heal us as individuals. In 1989, as I hiked in the mountains with my friend Gina, I clearly received a message that I was going to meet the man I was going to marry within a month. At the same time, I felt the most startling sensation: there was tingling radiating down my arms and into my chest, which it filled with a humming energy. The vibration traveled throughout my body, down my arms and into my fingertips, pulsing and buzzing. I shared this vision and experience with Gina and, both being rather cynical, we laughed at the absurdity of the experience because I wasn't even dating anyone at the time, let alone thinking about marriage.

Three weeks later, back in Canada, I started a new job and was taking part in a workshop. After everybody was already seated, the door opened again and a man entered. As soon as he walked towards me, I started feeling the same sensations I had experienced three weeks before in the mountains: the tingling, radiating, and pulsating down my arms and fingertips and into my chest. It was uncanny, wild—and completely absurd, especially since the person before me seemed very young and not at all somebody I could see myself in partnership with. I was amazed by my reaction: I had never had such a strong response to a person before (or since, for that matter). I watched this encounter in amazement, detached yet more alive than ever before.

Now I know that the body comes alive when the soul is ready, and the soul shows the way before the mind has even grasped what is happening. My brain was mocking the experience, saying, "Yeah, right, I'm not seriously thinking of dating anyone, let alone marrying." But to my credit, I did not close the door. I resisted the urge to discount my experience, so my pathways stayed clear and the mystery could unfold as it was meant to. I was open to the idea that my soul knew something my brain didn't. Our marriage took place in 1990.

*** Sensitives share helpful information from those who have passed over.**

You have already seen the healing power of this in my story of Navin's message to his grieving family.

*** Sensitives embody universal love.**

My first real experience of sensitive tenderness and universal love came when I held my newborn daughter for the first time. Later, when I let that sensitive tenderness expand and allowed the powerful positive forces in the universe to act through me, I entered an altered state of consciousness that became the catalyst for my own personal transformation. I can tell you with complete certainty that whenever we open to universal and unconditional love, wonderful things can happen.

Of course, every gift comes with its own particular set of challenges. Meeting and surmounting them is an ongoing process, but it is helpful to remember that perfection is not the goal, and that even in the midst of dealing with all the attendant difficulties, the gifts of Sensitivity shine like lights in the darkness.

The Challenges of Sensitivity

*** Sensitives can take on others' feelings.**

While a healthy Sensitive can understand another person's pain, but does not take it into herself, it can sometimes be difficult to shield ourselves from being overwhelmed by too much information. A sensitive person is obviously very receptive. We pick up on others' moods and we perceive signals of rejection very easily, and we often have a tendency to take those signals personally and take on the blame for causing anger, fear, etc. We need to learn to ask ourselves, "Is this mine, or is this someone else's?" Sometimes, during therapy with a client, I need to remind myself to be a neutral observer; a witness. Otherwise, I take on my client's pain or frustration which, of course, does not help anyone.

*** Strong negative feelings can interfere with your reception.**

Just as static can make a radio channel impossible to hear, so tumultuous emotions like anger, fear, and greed can drown out the voice of the Sensitive; intuition works best when the soul feels light, clear, and unencumbered by heavy thoughts. Perhaps this is why so many Sensitives access their information through dreams: when we are asleep, we are freed from our ordinary patterns of thought and perception, so we are able to access deeper levels of reality. It becomes a spiritual discipline when we are awake to keep ourselves clear of mucky feelings that interfere with our reception.

*** Sensitives can sometimes try to avoid their gift.**

Although we are all sensitive to a greater or a lesser degree, because there is such a societal disrespect for the gift, many of us find ourselves unable to embrace it. Then what happens? We may build a wall around ourselves and pretend our vulnerability doesn't exist. We may become sarcastic or defensive or work extra hard to overcome our perceived shortfalls. We may get into numbing and addictive behaviors to keep ourselves from being overwhelmed by too much stimulation. Or we may go into denial, pretending that a feeling isn't there—grief, for instance, which of course only succeeds in intensifying the sadness.

*** Sensitives are not honored by our culture.**

One of the greatest challenges of being a Sensitive is that society does not yet see our abilities as a gift. How many times have you heard "Don't be so sensitive"? This shaming has caused so much pain. In order to accomplish the shift that the world so desperately needs, sensitivity and its attendant intuition and receptiveness to spirit must be viewed as a valuable part of the human experience.

The Task at Hand

Our task is to harness the qualities of receptiveness and openness to Spirit, of sensitivity and intuition, and begin working with them consciously. It is a most joyful task: spirit-perceptiveness translates immediately into excitement, creating abundant energy that propels us forward, honoring the spirit and strengthening us hugely. Creative and inspired sensitivity is the most powerful gift we can bring to our own lives and to humanity.

All it takes is the desire to be a part of the solution rather than the problem, and the yearning to tap into and align yourself with the infinite loving energies of the universe.

Through the alignment with these energy sources you will be manifesting more and more of your deep soul desires. With this we we will raise our consciousness to the level of the heart, and the extraordinary power of healing energy can be accessed for the good of all.

Nurture Your Own Openness and Sensitivity

If you want to begin the process of owning and encouraging your sensitivity, here are some helpful practices to try:

Pay Attention

There are signs being shown to us every moment, but most of us are so intent on everyday reality that we fail to see them. When we open our inner eyes, we become aware of synchronicities and connections between things that are truly mind-blowing. When you receive messages, it is imperative to listen: it is our most important responsibility to be open and to learn who we really are. And don't worry: when you dwell in loving vibrations and the door to other worlds opens, you will feel safe and happy.

Trust Your Gut

Just for one day, try behaving as if the instinctual gut feelings you get are valid, true guidance from a wise inner part of yourself that is connected to the universal network. Check out the guidance with your mind: is it safe for yourself and others? Is it appropriate? If the answer is "yes," then follow it.

Journaling

I have found writing to be one valuable way of helping me to reclaim my centre. You may want to keep a journal, if you're not already doing so, to record your impressions, your hunches and intuitions, your struggles, and your triumphs. Record your own transformation. Observe how things change when you open to love, truth, honesty, connecting, oneness and infinity. Capture those key moments when a choice, decision, or response changed everything and brought you to a different level of consciousness. Write about your own divine coincidences. Then tell us your story: your energy is meant to inspire others. Stories are vehicles to transcend the current state. It is paramount for each of us to be part of the network that inspires, transcends, and moves the planet towards a more loving energy.

Try Some Deep Seeing

If you slow down and reflect on an image that attracts your attention you can learn more about yourself. Many people use Tarot cards for this, because the images are so rich and archetypal, but almost any image will yield some truth about you if you take the time to look. Take a picture that attracts you and really pay attention to it. What are the first three things you notice? Write them down. Now ask yourself, "What does this tell me about myself? In what way do these details relate to my life?" The more conscious and knowledgeable you are about yourself, the more your relationship to violence, sex, or love will change over time.

Nourishing Solitude

Finding time and space to be alone on a regular basis can be extraordinarily helpful. Sometimes it just takes a few minutes of inner quiet time to recharge. Often in the morning or at night, I find that time. I relax deeply, close my eyes and focus in on my heart centre of gratitude and appreciation. I let everything fall away, feeling a deep sense of coming home. This is wonderfully rejuvenating.

The Color Exercise

Visualizing color is one way to relax your mind so that the channel is freed up and the healing power of the universe can flow through. We can use color as a means of stilling our thoughts and listening with our inner ears and seeing with our inner eyes.

When I took a Jungian psychology class for my Master's degree, I explored the effects that different colors had on me while I was in deep meditation.

> Yellow was a beautiful experience for me, tranquil and fluid, sensual, bright and soft. I felt confident.
>
> Orange gave me great activity and energy, an expressive confidence.
>
> With red I changed from anger to a powerful strength and then to deep love.
>
> In green I had a real sense of community with people and nature and a profound feeling of sadness. This sadness was

connected to my grandfather's death. He was part of my "green world" of trees and meadows.

Blue I experienced as a crystal cave with diamonds, kings and queens surrounding me.

Indigo started as the scariest experience but the most important for my transformation. It was related to my own death. Here too, the usefulness of experiencing something as deeply as possible becomes apparent. When I allowed myself to go deeper into indigo, the color transformed into white and I became very joyous and a feeling of deep spirituality and goodness overcame me. It was also connected to my femininity and it felt as if I had transcended the death of that part of myself.

I experienced violet as very gentle, soft, feminine and vulnerable.

You can try this exercise yourself. Choose a time and place where you can be quiet and alone, and spend a few moments visualizing each color in your mind. Write down any impressions you receive. They may be very different from mine!

The Calming Power of Nature

I can come home to my inner quiet when I walk by the ocean and smell the salty sea air. I find flowers and lose myself by standing by them and taking in their aromatic beauty. What places in nature are restorative for you? If you can't actually spend time there, go to them in your mind.

Dancing and Movement

I love to listen to music and lose myself in dancing to it. Even if the dancing is only in my mind, it brings me much joy. When I am preoccupied with difficulties in my life, these dance sessions restore me. Dancing out frustration was one of my great stress releases when I was in young adulthood. Now I mostly feel inspiring music internally and let myself flow with the rhythm or melody.

One of my clients, a healer herself, felt very inhibited as an adult when it came to moving her body in ways that she thought might be construed as promiscuous. When I helped her create a space where it was permissible to move with wild abandon and not be judged about it, she felt joyous and let her movements flow with the music. Now, many years later, she still attends a minimum of two dance classes a week, ranging from belly dance to the rumba.

Discover the power of movement yourself by putting on the kind of music that moves you. Let yourself feel the music and trust your body to express itself in motion to the music.

Theme Songs

Music is a big part of my family's life. We attend concerts, compare musical tastes and listen to each other's preferences. I am proud of my daughter's fine sense of music appreciation. If I am overwhelmed by too many everyday duties I know what will bring me out of my struggles: I listen to what I call my theme songs: *Imagine* by John Lennon is one of them. These songs calm and inspire me by resonating with who I am. What songs resonate for you? Which ones fill you with hope and serenity and inspiration? Make it a practice to listen to them whenever you need to.

The Practice of Love

To feel whole I need to tune into love first and foremost, every day. I need to feel the love for the people most precious in my life. I also need to feel their love for me. If you know you are loved, everything is easier. Spend time every day holding those you love in your thoughts.

A Word About Indigo Children

Much has been written lately about Indigo children, those children who know how to live creatively, and communicate on a light grid that allows for telepathic communications amongst themselves. They are confident about a global vision of brother and sisterhood that transcends all separation between sexes, orientations, races, and religions. Unfortunately, they also are prone to addictions, can be frustrated and bored easily, don't fit into most conventional school programs, and are often diagnosed with ADD. They are very sensitive, although they not easily influenced and don't like authority. They can be living examples of love in action but when they feel blocked, they can show rather narcissistic tendencies and behave like royalty.

Some people have predicted that we will move from having a two-stranded double helix in the DNA to a 12-stranded helix or more. Apparently there is now some scientific proof that we are changing at this level. On the web, I found an interview with Dr. Berranda Fox, a physiologist and naturopath. She said that in Mexico City several years ago there was a convention of geneticists from around the world, and the main topic was the DNA change. It was apparent that humans are making an evolutionary change, but we don't yet know what we are changing into. The changes are not being made public, because the scientific community feels it would frighten the population. Dr. Fox knows that we are changing at the cellular level: she is presently working with three children who have three-stranded DNA helixes! She believes it is a positive mutation even though it can be misunderstood and frightening physically, mentally, and emotionally .

Successfully raising indigo children is clearly one of the positive steps on the path to the new paradigm. The general practices below can give you some helpful advice.

General Practices for Living in the Emerging Paradigm

The more of these actions you take on a daily basis, the more clearly you will find yourself having shifted to New Paradigm Living. I came up with this list when thinking about how to help our children thrive but, interestingly, it is also a way for all of us to learn to be with each other authentically.

1. Develop nurturing behavior by:

   Inviting questions, asking questions and listening for the answer.

   Looking for and appreciating the positive intention in other's messages.

   Sharing power and apologizing when you have been wrong.

2. Model expressing emotions healthily:

Talk them out.

Speak about your own feelings instead of laying blame.

Work off your anger by doing something constructive.

Deal with the problem when you have cooled down.

Then develop solutions if possible together, which will create a win-win scenario.

3. Take one thing at a time; lighten up, and allow yourself to make an occasional mistake.

4. Look at your mistakes as an opportunity to learn.

5. Do something for someone else:

   It helps get your mind of your own problem, by putting them into perspective. It gives your life purpose and value when you can serve humanity well.

   It creates win-win scenarios, power of intention, and opens you to divine guidance.

6. Schedule time for fun with each other and by yourself.

7. Stop judging, avoiding, blaming, punishing, overprotecting, demanding, controlling, withholding, labeling, and arguing. After the initial satisfaction of venting and feeling vindicated, you feel even more frustrated and end up in ruminating, justifying your thoughts to lead to another bout of the same behavior. That is a self-defeating self-perpetuating mechanism and originates from the old paradigm. Instead find a way to set limits

and use consequences which you can reinforce. Being spirited is not a license to let children or others control you. Teach and model coping skills and resilience and reinforce your children and other loved ones when they use them.

As We Go Forward

> *"Any intelligent fool can make things bigger, more complex, and more violent. It takes a touch of genius - and a lot of courage - to move in the opposite direction."*
>
> —Albert Einstein

Obviously, a paradigm shift does not happen overnight. It is a process, and just like the process of accepting loss, there are stages we go through. First we are in shock or denial about how the popular opinion could have been wrong. Then we get sad or angry: "This new paradigm stuff doesn't work, it's a bunch of boloney." We give up, and go right on doing all the self-defeating things that keep us sad or angry. Then comes a period of resignation, when we hit rock bottom; we realize our habitual ways of being aren't working, either—and a willingness to try something new emerges. This is when we put a toe in the water, gradually doing more and more as we see that the new ways actually do make us happier. Soon we realize there really is something to all this and we begin to own our courage and accept the shift in thinking and attitudes. Eventually, we really see results—and by that point, we have actually made the shift and we can be a part of the tipping point. That's when the mass is reached to create a field large enough and powerful enough to attract more of the same positive energy.

My dreams and guidance showed me that I needed to write this book for many reasons, but one was to change women's sense of self worth, to teach us about listening to inner guidance and emotions, expanding our creative and intuitive capacities, living our lives with grace, joy, and compassion, while gaining wisdom to help ourselves and our families. I was told that both men and women need to awaken their hearts and spirits and surrender to love, and that there is a roadmap for overcoming obstacles in relationships, cultivating joy, and opening the door to a fearless existence.

Deepak Chopra teaches us that there are "infinite realms of consciousness beyond waking, dreaming and sleeping, with the straight lines of time as threads of a web extending to infinity." This rings profoundly true to me as I look back on my own discoveries, which have essentially become this book.

I have often heard it said that women could save the world, but I don't think the job applies so much to women as a gender as to the qualities of receptivity and openness. Yes, these are the qualities of the deep feminine, the feminine essence, but they can just as easily be expressed by men and children. Remaining open to pleasure, messages, kindness, the rewards we all want, is not a uniquely female trait or ability. We simply need to open and spontaneously appreciate instead of criticizing.

When we stay open, we heed our sensitivity, and when we heed our sensitivity, we stay open. With this attitude of open awareness, we realize the abundant richness of life. We start looking deeply at music, art and literature, as well as practices for peace of mind, like meditation, and life becomes a wondrous adventure.

Making the decision to generate more positive power to counter negativity is a good start for anybody. From this place it is possible to tap into love, the most powerful positive energy in the universe. It is waiting for you, and for us collectively, for no matter how we all vary, we are all connected. We are all one.

Bibliography

Books

Albion, Mark. *Making a Life, Making a Living: Reclaiming Your Purpose and Passion in Business and in Life*. New York, NY: Warner Books, 2000.

Ball, Pamela. *The Complete Dream Dictionary*. Etobicoke, ON: Prospero Books, 1999.

Bassett Lucinda. *From Panic to Power: Proven Techniques to Calm your Anxieties, Conquer your Fears, and Put you in Control of your Life*. New York, NY: Harper Collins, 1995.

Ban Breathnach, Sarah. *Something More: Excavating Your Authentic Self*. New York, NY: Warner Books, 1998.

(As told to) Booth, Stephanie. "Your True Life Story: I have Psychic Powers." *Teen People*, June/July 2005, p. 82.

Braden, Gregg. *The God Code: The Secret of Our Past, the Promise of Our Future*. Carlsbad, CA: Hay House, 2004.

Browne, Sylvia. *Conversations with the Other Side*. Carlsbad, CA: Hay House, 2002.

Browne, Sylvia. *God, Creation, and Tools for Life*. Carlsbad, CA: Hay House, 2000.

Browne, Sylvia. *The Nature of Good and Evil.* Carlsbad, CA: Hay House, 2001.

Browne, Sylvia. *Book of Dreams.* New York, NY: Penguin Books, 2002.

Cameron, Julia. *Walking in this World: The Practical Art of Creativity,* New York, NY Penguin, 2002.

Carroll, Lee. *Partnering with God: Practical Information for the New Millennium.* Del Mar, CA: Kryon, 1997.

Chopra Deepak. *The Way of the Wizard: Twenty Spiritual Lessons in Creating the Life You Want.* New York, NY: Harmony Books, 1995.

Coloroso, Barbara. *The Bully, the Bullied, and the Bystander.* Lecture in March 2004..

Colton, Ann Ree. *Watch Your Dreams.* Glendale, CA: ARC Publishing, 1973.

Covey, Sean. *The 7 Habits of Highly Effective Teens.* New York, NY: Simon & Schuster, 1998.

Cox, Simon. *Cracking the DaVinci Code: The Unauthorized Guide to the Facts Behind Dan Brown's Bestselling Novel.* New York, NY. Sterling, 2004.

Day, Malcolm. *The Book of Miracles: Extraordinary Events in Ordinary Lives*. Hauppauge, NY: Barron's, 2002.

Day, Peggy and Susan Gale. *Edgar Cayce on the Indigo Children: Understanding Psychic Children*. Virginia Beach, VA: A.R.E. Press, 2004.

Dyer, Dr. Wayne W. *The Power of Intention: Learning to Co-create Your World Your Way*. Carlsbad, CA: Hay House, 2004.

Eker, T. Harv *The Millionaire Mind*. Workshop May 2005. www.peakpotentials.com

Emoto, Dr. Masuro, *The Hidden Messages from Water*, Vol I and II. Hillsboro, OR, Beyond Words Publishing, 2004.

Fraser, Sylvia. *The Book of Strange: A Journey*. Toronto, ON: Doubleday, 1992.

Gelb, Michael J. *DaVinci Decoded: Discovering the Spiritual Secrets of Leonardo's Seven Principles.* New York, NY. Delacorte Press, 2004.

Goldberg, Natalie. *Writing Down the Bones: Freeing the Writer Within*. Boston, MA: Shambhala Publications, 1986.

Goldher Lerner, Dr. Harriett. *The Dance of Anger*. New York, N.Y: Harper & Row Publishers,1985.

Greive, Bradley Trevor. *Tomorrow: Adventures in an Uncertain World*. Kansas City, Missouri: McMeel Publishing, 2003.

Hart, George. *Ancient Egypt*. London, GB. Dorling Kindersley, 1990

Hayakawa, Ellen. *The Inspired Organization: Spirituality and Energy at Work*. Victoria, BC: Trafford Publishing, 2003.

Hay L. Louise. *Heal Your Body*. Carson, CA: Hay House, 1982.

Hawkins, Dr. David R. *Power vs. Force: The Hidden Determinants of Human Behavior*. Carlsbad, CA: Hay House, 2002.

Jampolsky, Dr. Gerald G. *Mini Course for Healing Relationships and Bringing about Peace of Mind*. Tiburon, CA: Foundation for Inner Peace, 1979

Kurcinka, Mary Sheedy. *Raising your Spirited Child*. New York, NY: Harper Collins, 1991.

Lynch, Amy with Dr. Linda Ashford. *How Can You* Say *That?* Middleton, WI: Pleasant Company Publications, 2003.

Melchizedek Drunvalo *The Ancient Secret of the Flower of Life (Volume 1)*, Flagstaff, AZ.: Light Technology Publishing, 1990.

Millman, Dan. *The Life You Were Born to Live: A Guide to Finding Your Life Purpose*. Tiburon, CA: H J Kramer, 1993.

Nadler, Spencer. The *Language of Cells: Life as Seen Under the Microscope*. New York, NY: Random House, 2001.

Northrop, Suzane. *Second Chance: Healing Messages from the Afterlife*. San Diego, CA: Jodere Group, 2002.

Neufeld, Dr. Gordon and Mate Dr. Gabor. *Hold on to your Kids: Why Parents need to Matter more than Peers*. Toronto, Ontario: Vintage Canada, 2005

Orloff, Dr. Judith. *Dr. Judith Orloff's Guide to Intuitive Healing: Five Steps to Physical, Emotional, and Sexual Wellness*. New York, NY: Times Books, 2000.

Restak, Dr. Richard. *Mozart's Brain and the Fighter Pilot: Unleashing Your Brain's Potential*. New York, NY: Harmony Books, 2001.

Richardson, Cheryl. *The Unmistakable Touch of Grace*. New York, NY: Free Press, 2005.

Sheldrake Rupert. *The Sense of Being Stared At*. New York, NY: Crown Publishers, 2003.

Scholl Inge, *The White Rose*, Wesleyan University Press, New England, Hanover, NH 03755, 1970.

Shreeve, James. "Corina's Brain all she is…is here." *National Geographic*, March, 2005, p.6.

Shreeve, James. "Spiritual State." *National Geographic Magazine*, March 2005, p. 31.

Shuter, Jane. *Ancient Egypt: Discoveries & Inventions*. Des Plaines, IL. Heinemann Library, 1999

Stearn, Jess. *Intimates through Time: Edgar Cayce's Mysteries of Reincarnation*. New York, NY: Signet, 1993.

Stuyt, Sharka www.ExecutiveLifeCoach.com, *Make it Happen*! Workshop June 2005

Talbot, Michael. *The Holographic Universe*. New York, NY: Harper Perennial, 1992

Temple-Thurston, Leslie and Brad Laughlin. *Marriage of Spirit: Enlightened Living in Today's World*. Santa Fe, NM: CoreLight Publishing, 2000.

Ueland, Brenda. *If You Want to Write*. Saint Paul, MN: Graywolf Press, 1987.

Van De Castle, Robert L. *Our Dreaming Mind: A Sweeping Exploration of the Role That Dreams Have Played in Politics, Art, Religion, and Psychology, from Ancient Civilizations to the Present Day*. New York, NY: Random House, 1994.

Warren, Rick. *The Purpose-Driven Life: What on Earth am I Here For?* Grand Rapids, MI: Zondervan, 2002.

Wiseman, Rosalind. *Queen Bees and Wannabes: Helping Your Daughter Survive Cliques, Gossip, Boyfriends, and Other Realities of Adolescence.* New York, NY: Three Rivers Press, 2002.

Yamamoto, Gary K. *Creative Dream Analysis: A Guide to Self-Development*. Avenel, NJ. Wing Books, 1995.

Zukav, Gary. *The Dancing Wu Li Masters: An overview of the New Physics.* San Francisco, CA. William Morrow and Company, 1979.

Zukav, Gary. *The Seat of the Soul.* NY: A Fireside Book, Simon & Schuster Inc., 1990.

Zukav, Gary. *Soul Stories.* New York, NY: Fireside, 2000.

DVD

David Suzuki, *Documentary: Suzuki Speaks.* The Spiritual Cinema Circle, 2005 - Volume 2, Directed by Tony Papa. www.SpiritualCinemaCircle.com

Websites

Fox, Dr. Berrenda."DNA Changes," Notes from Dr. Fox in Mt. Shasta, 30 Mar 2002.
http://www.globalpsychics.com/lp/Prophecy/children_light.htm#dna

Talbot, Michael. *The Holographic Universe.*
http://www/crystalinks.com/holographic.html.
Accessed 29/11/2004

What the Bleep Do We Know, www.whatthebleep.com

Wisdom Children: "The New Children: A Call to Service," WisdomChildren@earthlink.net. Accessed June 14, 2005.

Recommended Reading

Ball, Pamela. *The Complete Dream Dictionary*. Etobicoke, ON: Prospero Books, 1999.

Bassett Lucinda. *From Panic to Power: Proven Techniques to Calm your Anxieties, Conquer your Fears, and Put you in Control of your Life*. New York, NY: Harper Collins, 1995.

Browne, Sylvia. *The Nature of Good and Evil*. Carlsbad, CA: Hay House, 2001.

Browne, Sylvia. *Book of Dreams*. New York, NY: Penguin Books, 2002.

Chapman, Dr.Gary. *The Five Love Languages*. Chicago, IL: Northfield Publishing, 1995.

Chopra Deepak. *The Seven Spiritual Laws of Success* . San Francisco, CA: Amber-Allen, 2007.

Covey Stephen R. *7 Habits Family Collection: Leadership Where it Matters Most*. Gildan Media Corp., New York: Gildan Audio, 2005

Dyer, Dr. Wayne W. *The Power of Intention: Learning to Co-create Your World Your Way*. Carlsbad, CA: Hay House, 2004.

Goldher Lerner, Dr. Harriett. *The Dance of Anger*. New York, N.Y: Harper & Row Publishers,1985.

Hay L. Louise. *Heal Your Body*. Carson, CA: Hay House, 1982.

Hawkins, Dr. David R. *Power vs. Force: The Hidden Determinants of Human Behavior*. Carlsbad, CA: Hay House, 2002.
Orloff, Dr. Judith. *Dr. Judith Orloff's Guide to Intuitive Healing: Five Steps to Physical, Emotional, and Sexual Wellness*. New York, NY: Times Books, 2000.

Orloff, Dr. Judith. *Second Sight*. New York, NY: Warner Books, 1996.

Ruiz, Don Miguel. *The Four Agreements: A Practical Guide to Personal Freedom*. San Francisco, CA: Amber Allen Publishing, 2001.

Sheldrake Rupert. *The Sense of Being Stared At*. New York, NY: Crown Publishers, 2003.

Talbot, Michael. *The Holographic Universe*. New York, NY: Harper Perennial, 1992

Van De Castle, Robert L. *Our Dreaming Mind: A Sweeping Exploration of the Role That Dreams Have Played in Politics, Art, Religion, and Psychology, from Ancient Civilizations to the Present Day*. New York, NY: Random House, 1994.

Wiseman, Rosalind. *Queen Bees and Wannabes: Helping Your Daughter Survive Cliques, Gossip, Boyfriends, and Other Realities of Adolescence*. New York, NY: Three Rivers Press, 2002.

Yamamoto, Gary K. *Creative Dream Analysis: A Guide to Self-Development*. Avenel, NJ. Wing Books, 1995.

Zukav, Gary. *The Dancing Wu Li Masters: An Overview of the New Physics*. San Francisco, CA. William Morrow and Company, 1979.

Printed in the United States
93446LV00005B/1-201/A

9 780979 882807